Introduction to Islam for Malawi

Copyright 2021 David Bone

All rights reserved. No part of this publication may be reproduced, stored in a retrieval system, or transmitted in any form or by any means, electronic, mechanical, photocopying, recording or otherwise without prior permission from the publishers.

Published by

Mzuni Press

P/Bag 201, Mzuzu 2, Malawi

ISBN   978-99960-60-90-8

eISBN   978-99960-60-91-5

Mzuni Press is represented outside Malawi by:

African Books Collective Oxford (order@africanbookscollective.com)

www.africanbookscollective.com

www.mzunipress.blogspot.com

Cover design: David Bone, Klaus Fiedler and Josephine Kawejere
Cover map: Dr Michael R. Izady. The Gulf/2000 Project-SIPA-Columbia University, by kind permission of the author.
Cover picture: Tsanko Madinga Kasambala.

Introduction to Islam for Malawi

David Bone

Mzuni Books no. 47

Mzuzu

2021

Glossary

al-fatiha (Arabic)	the opening (initial chapter of the Qur'an)
abd (Arabic)	servant
adhan (Arabic)	call to prayer
aya (Arabic)	verse (of the Qur'an)
baraka (Arabic)	blessing
dhikr (Arabic)	remembrance (of the name of God)
dhimmi (Arabic)	protected minority
Eid ul-Adha (Arabic)	Feast of Sacrifice
Eid ul-Fitr (Arabic)	festival ending Ramadan
fatwa (Arabic)	legally binding declaration
fiqh (Arabic)	understanding (about Islamic legal rulings from sources)
Hadith (Arabic)	report/s (about actions and words of the Prophet)
Hajj (Arabic)	obligatory pilgrimage
halal (Arabic)	permitted
haram (Arabic)	prohibited
haqiqa (Arabic)	truth
hijab (Arabic)	modest Muslim covering
hijrah (Arabic)	emigration (of Muslims from Medina to Mecca)
Ifriqiya (Arabic)	area included in modern day Libya, Tunisia and Algeria
ijaza (Arabic)	authorization to transmit religious knowledge
imam (Arabic)	leader
Injil (Arabic)	Gospel
jando (Yao)	Yao boys' Islamized initiation ceremony

jihad (Arabic)	striving (in the way of God)
jizya (Arabic)	tax on 'protected minorities'
jumbe (Swahili)	governor/chief/sultan
lupanda (Yao)	Yao boys' traditional initiation ceremony
madrassa (Arabic)	school
Mahdi (Arabic)	the expected one
masjid (Arabic)	mosque
mu'alim (Arabic)	teacher
Maulid (Arabic)	birthday (of the Prophet)
Muhajirun (Arabic)	emigrants
mwalimu (Swahili)	religious teacher
nabi (Arabic)	prophet
qadi (Arabic)	judge
qiyas (Arabic)	process of deductive analogy
raab (Arabic)	master
Rashidun (Arabic)	rightly guided (Caliphs)
rasul (Arabic)	prophet
ribat (Arabic)	stronghold
sadaka (Yao)	Yao Muslim funerary rite
sadaqa (Arabic)	voluntary charitable giving
Salat (Arabic)	obligatory prayers
Saum (Arabic)	obligatory fasting
Shahada (Arabic)	declaration of faith
sikili (Yao)	dance with religious origins
Sunna (Arabic)	the way of the Prophet
sura (Arabic)	chapter (of the Qur'an)
tariqa (Arabic)	lit. way: a Sufi order
Tawrat (Arabic)	Torah
Ulema (Arabic)	class of learned Muslim scholars
Umma (Arabic)	the community of Muslims

Umrah (Arabic)	minor pilgrimage
wali (Arabic)	authorized agent
wazir (Arabic)	minister
Zabur (Arabic)	Psalms
Zakat (Arabic)	obligatory almsgiving
ziyara (Arabic)	lit. visit: in Malawi, ceremony for the Prophet's birthday

Contents

Glossary	4
Foreword	14
Introduction	
Why Study Islam?	16
Purpose and Structure of the Book	18

SECTION 1: THE FOUNDATIONS OF ISLAM

Part 1: The Prophet — 22

Chapter 1

The Seal of the Prophets	22
The Qur'an and the Bible	23

Chapter 2

The Arabian Setting	26
The Land and the People	26
The Religious Background	28

Chapter 3

The Early Life of Muhammad	32
The Night of Power	33
The Revelations	34

Chapter 4

Proclaiming the Message	36
Early Reaction in Mecca	36
Opposition in Mecca	37
Persecution	39

Chapter 5

Muhammad in Medina — 41
- The Hijrah — 41
- Establishing the Community of Islam — 42
- Muhammad and the Jewish tribes — 44

Chapter 6

Conflict with the Quraysh — 47
- The Battle of Badr — 47
- The Battle of Uhud — 48
- Expansion and Consolidation — 49

Chapter 7

Muhammad Wins Mecca — 52
- The Treaty of al-Hudaybiyyah — 52
- The Capture of Mecca — 53
- Muhammad's Final Years — 54
- Muhammad's Legacy — 55

THE FOUNDATIONS OF ISLAM
Part 2: The Book — 57

Chapter 8

The Qur'an — 57
- The Divisions of the Qur'an — 58
- The Compilation of the Qur'an — 58

Chapter 9

The Teaching about God in the Qur'an — 60
- The Unity of God — 60
- God as Creator and Sustainer — 61

God's Sovereign Will	62

Chapter 10

The Teaching of the Qur'an about Humankind	63
People Dependent on God	63
How People should Respond to God	64
Right-doing	65

Chapter 11

The Teaching of the Qur'an about Judgement, Paradise and Hell	67
The Day of Judgement	67
Paradise	68
Hell	69

THE FOUNDATIONS OF ISLAM

Part 3: Islamic Law and Guidance   **70**

Chapter 12

Regulating the Community	70
The First two Sources of Authority	71
Hadith	72

Chapter 13

The Scholars of Islam, the *Ulema*	75
The Sources of Authority of Islamic Law	76

Chapter 14

The Obligations of Islam	80
The Religious Obligations	80
Prayer	80
Almsgiving	81
Fasting	82

Pilgrimage	82
Social and Economic Obligations	84

SECTION 2
DEVELOPMENT AND DIVERSITY — 86

Chapter 15
The Rightly Guided Caliphs — 86
Abu Bakr	86
Umar	88
Uthman	90
Ali	91

Chapter 16
Diversity within Islam — 93
The Shia	94
Diversity within Shi-ism	96

Chapter 17
The Development of Islamic Theology — 100
The Mutazilites	100

Chapter 18
The Development of Islamic Theology II — 104
The Reply of the Orthodox	104
The Arguments of al-Ashari	105

Chapter 19
The Sufis I — 108
Origins	108
Developments	110

Chapter 20
The Sufis II — 112
- A Challenge to Orthodoxy — 112
- Al-Ghazali — 113
- The Brotherhoods — 115

SECTION 3
ISLAM COMES TO AFRICA AND TO MALAWI — 117

Chapter 21
Islam comes to North Africa — 117
- Initial Conquest — 117
- Independence from Control of the Caliphs — 118
- The Fatimid Dynasty — 119

Chapter 22
Reform Movements in North Africa — 121
- The Almoravids — 121
- The Almohads — 122

Chapter 23
Muslims in West Africa, the First Thousand Years — 124
- The Empire of Ghana — 124
- The Empire of Mali — 125
- The Empire of Songhai — 126

Chapter 24
Muslims in West Africa, the Great Reformers — 128
- Uthman dan Fodio — 129
- Al-Hajj Umar — 130

Chapter 25
Muslims in East Africa, the First Thousand Years — 132
- The Shirazi Era — 134
- The Portuguese Disruption — 135
- The Omani Era — 135

Chapter 26
Muslims Come to the Interior of East Africa — 138
- Early Contacts — 138
- The Growth and Spread of Islam — 140
- Implications for the Development of Islam — 141

Chapter 27
The Establishment of Islam in Malawi — 143
- The Jumbes — 144
- The Yao — 145
- European Opposition — 146
- Chiefs and Shaykhs — 147
- Islamic Practice in this Period — 148

Chapter 28
Education and Revival — 151
- Muslims and Western Education — 151
- Independence — 152
- Revival and Development — 154
- Reactions — 156

Chapter 29
A Muslim President, 1994-2004 — 157
- Changes — 158

Education and Development	159
Malawi's Muslims and Wider Society	161
Chapter 30	
Muslims in Malawi 2004-2020	165
Education and Development	166
Desire for a Muslim Friendly Society	167
Unity in diversity	169
Suggestions for Further Reading	172
Online Resources	173

Foreword

The origin of this book is a course of lectures introducing the study of Islam to students at Chancellor College, St. Peter's Major Seminary and Zomba Theological College between 1977 and 1987. The contents have been completely revised and added to, in the light of what I have learned from researching, studying and teaching the subject in the more than thirty years since then.

If parts of this book seem familiar to some readers it is because a copy of my original lecture notes was incorporated, with neither my knowledge nor consent, into a book entitled 'Beliefs and Practices of Muslims: the religion of our neighbours'. It included an introductory chapter and other sections, not written by me and that in no way reflect my views.

I welcome the invitation of the Editor-in-Chief of Mzuni Press, Prof Klaus Fiedler, to write this book and gratefully acknowledge his invaluable help in its production.

Writing about a religion, especially a religion other than one's own, requires a great deal of care not to misrepresent it. Consequently, I am extremely grateful to Dr Alhagi Manta Drammeh, Associate Professor of Islamic Studies at Al-Maktoum College Dundee, with long experience of teaching non-Muslim students about Islam, who has kindly read the text and has been of great help with suggestions and corrections. I of course take sole responsibility for any inadvertent errors, misinterpretations or other shortcomings that may remain.

I would also like to thank Dr Patricia Kelly of St. Andrews University for proof-reading and checking passages for intelligibility, and Emeritus Professor Antony Black of

Dundee University for encouragement and helpful comments on the text.

Introduction

Why Study Islam?

A study of Islam has rightly become an integral part of the curriculum of departments of Religious Studies, Theological Colleges and Teacher Training Colleges in Malawi. Given the importance of the religion in so many ways, it is also worthy of the attention of a much wider reading public, for a number of reasons.

Firstly, there is the sheer number of Muslims throughout the world. As of 2020 one and a half billion people, almost a quarter of the world's population, profess that there is no god except Allah and that Muhammad is His Prophet. Of all the world's faiths, only Christianity has more followers. Secondly there are the many different ways in which Islam has had, and continues to have, an influence on the world both for Muslims and the rest of humanity.

Worldwide, Muslims form the majority of the population in over forty nations. Some, like Indonesia, Pakistan, Bangladesh, Egypt and Turkey are amongst the twenty most populous in the world. Some, like Saudi Arabia and the Gulf States, are among the world's most economically powerful. Nine out of the twelve members of the Organisation of the Oil Producing and Exporting Countries (OPEC) have Muslim majorities. Some countries including Saudi Arabia, Pakistan, and Iran are officially Muslim states whose constitutions, institutions and laws are explicitly founded on Islamic principles. In all countries with a Muslim majority, in one way or another, Islam exercises a strong influence on politics, values, customs and culture. Many countries in Europe, North America and Asia have significant Muslim minorities.

In Africa, the lands north of the Sahara have long been solidly part of the Islamic world, with Arabic as the official language, or one of them, and very large Muslim majorities. From there Muslims have taken their faith southwards, down the Nile to Sudan and across the Sahara to the northern part of West Africa. In both of these areas Muslims are substantially in the majority and Islam is a major influence on culture, identity, law and politics. Along the east coast of Africa as far south as northern Mozambique, the mingling of Muslim Arabs and Persians with local Bantu inhabitants has produced a new people, the Swahili, with a new language and culture. Some countries in Africa, such as Nigeria, have almost equal numbers of Christians and Muslims. There are relatively few countries on the continent which do not have a significant minority of Muslims.

In Malawi, where Islam arrived before Christianity, a substantial minority of the population are Muslims and, in some areas, they form the majority. Many people in one major ethnic group, the Yao, have an especially close association with the religion. In cities and many areas of the country the distinctive presence of Islam can be seen in the form of mosques, ways of dressing, customs and festivals. Muslims have provided Malawi with a State President and Vice-President, Cabinet Ministers and Ambassadors, as well as leading figures in commerce, the professions and the security services.

While religion is only one of very many factors which influence current affairs, locally, nationally and internationally, an informed and accurate understanding of the Islamic factor is extremely important. Where there is a lack of information, or even worse, misinformation or misrepresentation, it becomes easier for prejudices to be confirmed or become established, and for these prejudices to be exploited by people with a particular political or religious agenda to cause fear, enmity and division.

Knowledge and understanding of what people believe, value and aspire to is especially important for religious leaders, both Christian and Muslim, whose responsibility is to guide their flocks in encouraging them to live godly lives, give faithful witness and to work for harmony and justice in society. This is not always easy when both Christianity and Islam are religions which claim to be universally valid and whose followers are commissioned to commend their faith to others. The difficulty is often compounded by a legacy of hostility and mistrust between representatives of the two religions over the centuries and up to the present day.

This knowledge and understanding is also extremely important for political leaders and policy makers who have the responsibility of keeping their countries united and harnessing the skills and energies of all its peoples. It is also important for all teachers and people in the media whose task it is to inform and to mould opinion, so that those who read, watch, listen and learn are fed with accurate and balanced information. This is all the more vital as there has been a tendency in many countries for the people of the majority religion, whether Christianity or Islam, to be given a distorted and fearful picture of the other faith and its peoples, and for members of the minority religion, with an equally incomplete and inaccurate image of the other religion and its members, to feel persecuted and marginalized.

Purpose and Structure of the Book

This book aims to contribute to knowledge and understanding in three main ways and falls into three sections. First and foremost, it offers a concise introduction to the foundations on which the religion of Islam is based. It then goes on to describe the expansion and development of the Islamic Community and account for some of the sources of the rich diversity that is found among Muslims. Some of this diversity comes from the very different cultures in which Islam has found a place, and some of it comes also from different interpretations of the foundations of the religion itself. The book concludes with an outline of how Islam has come to Africa, and to Malawi in particular, and how it has found expression in the lives of Muslims there.

By way of explaining the foundations, the first part starts with a brief explanation of what lies at the very heart of Islam, the belief that God is God alone and that Muhammad is His prophet. It then goes on to give an account of the life of the Prophet. This section of the book begins by looking briefly at Arabia in the time of Muhammad, the country in which he was born and in which his career took place, and at the Arab people, of whom he was one, and to whom he came to believe that he had been sent by God. It then goes on to give an account of Muhammad's life and prophetic career; his early days in Mecca, the start of the revelations he believed were from God, and how these were received by people in his city, his emigration to the city of Medina and his setting up of the Islamic Community there, conflict with his opponents and his final winning over of Mecca and the whole of Arabia.

The next part has its focus on the Qur'an itself; its contents, its structure, how it was compiled, and the teaching of its main themes; about God, about humankind, and about the judgement to come. This is followed in a third part by an account of the ways in which Muslims, led by their learned scholars, have developed a code of guidance and regulations, the *Shariah*, to ensure that they, as individuals and as a Community, are living in obedience to God's will. It examines the sources of authority on which this code is based and explains the Schools of Law which worked out its details. This section then goes on to set out some of the main religious duties laid out in the *Shariah* as well as some of the most important social and economic obligations it contains.

The era of the Muhammad's first four successors, the 'Rightly Guided Caliphs' is looked back on by Muslims as a most important and formative time when, under righteous leaders, their Community spread rapidly and was at its purest. However, it was also during this time that the seeds of diversity were sown. This second section of the book gives an account of the rule and achievements of each of these four Caliphs and also of the first political splits and religious disagreements. It goes on to give a brief description and explanation of the origins, development and features of the main group to separate itself from the major Sunni Community, the Shia branch of Islam, and to give an account of the main divisions within the Shia themselves.

The next two chapters attempt to explain how different schools of Muslim theologians have worked out answers to questions about how God should be understood and how His will for humankind can be known. It outlines some of the main controversies that arose, and the attempts that were made to resolve them.

Another source of diversity within Islam has been that between people who have given priority to knowing about God and doing His will, and groups of Muslims, the Sufis, who have attempted to find a more personal experience of Him. Two chapters explain the origins, development and the features of the Sufi movement and the Brotherhoods like the Qadiriyya and Shadhiliyya, that have arisen out of it.

How Islam has come to Africa, and to Malawi in particular, and how it has found expression in people's lives there is the subject of the final section of the book. It offers an overview of the spread of Islam into North, West and East Africa, before modern times, highlighting some of the main movements, events and figures in this story in order to give some idea of the long history of Islam and the extent of its impact on these areas of the continent.

The section ends in Malawi with an outline of how the religion was first brought to the country, by whom, and in what circumstances and in what ways it became established in certain areas and among certain groups of people. It also tries to account for some of the changes and developments that have taken place within Muslim communities in the different eras of Malawi's history up to the present day, the events and the forces that have brought them about and the place of Muslims in wider Malawian society.

There is an unfortunate human tendency which leads us to think that if we don't know about something it cannot be very important. It is my hope that this book might make a contribution to promoting knowledge and understanding of a most important subject, namely Islam, and some of the ways in which the influence of the religion has found expression in the values, attitudes and customs of those who profess it.

SECTION 1: THE FOUNDATIONS OF ISLAM

Part 1: The Prophet

Chapter 1

The Seal of the Prophets

There is no god but God and Muhammad is the Prophet of God. Muslim Creed.

Say you: "We believe in Allah, and the revelation given to us, and to Abraham, Ismai'l, Isaac, Jacob, and the Tribes and that given to Moses and Jesus, and that given to (all) Prophets from their Lord: we make no difference between one and another of them: and we bow to Allah (in Islam). Sura 2:136

Before looking at Muhammad's life in detail, an examination will be made of what Muslims mean by saying that Muhammad is the Prophet of God and that Muslims accept the message of all the prophets before Muhammad.

According to Muslim belief, prophets were men chosen by God to convey His message to mankind. Muslims do not believe that Muhammad was the first of God's prophets or indeed His only one. In Sura 46:9 of the Qur'an Muhammad is instructed to say, *I am no bringer of new fangled doctrine among the messengers.*

The belief is that human life on earth began with prophethood in that Adam, the first man, was also the first prophet. It is believed that God sent His prophets to all peoples at different times. According to one reckoning they total 124,000. Furthermore, it is believed that the message of each of them was the same, teaching the oneness of God and the judgement to come, and that it is the duty of all Muslims to believe the whole message of all the prophets.

> Those who deny Allah and His Messengers and (those who) wish to separate Allah from His Messengers, saying: "We believe in some but reject others": and (those who) wish to take a course midway, they are in truth (equally) unbelievers. Sura 4:150-151a

In the Qur'an twenty-eight prophets are mentioned by name and most of these are Biblical figures, including Nooh (Noah), Ishaq (Isaac), Yakub (Jacob), Musa (Moses), Ibrahim (Abraham), Yusuf (Joseph) and Isa (Jesus). Muslims differentiate between a prophet to whom written revelations were given, *rasul* and one to whom no revelations were given, *nabi*. The Qur'an refers to three written revelations before the Qur'an itself, the *Tawrat* (Torah) given to Moses, the *Zabur* (Psalms) given to David and the *Injil* (Gospel) given to Jesus.

The Qur'an and the Bible

The Christians and Jews in Arabia who heard this teaching, that all the prophets spoke the same message as was being revealed to Muhammad, objected that their scriptures did not correspond exactly with Muhammad's version of them. There were many points of difference for example between what the New Testament and Qur'an said about Jesus. The explanation that Muhammad, gave, on the basis of further revelations, was that over time the messages that had been given to Moses, David, and Jesus had become wilfully distorted by man-made additions, omissions, alterations and interpretations. The Muslim teaching is consequently that the Torah, Psalms and Gospels, in their present form, do not accurately reflect what they originally contained, but that if they did, they would agree completely with the message of the Qur'an.

For Muslims the importance of Muhammad as the prophet of God is that to him was given God's perfect and final message to humankind. The Qur'an is thus considered to be the most excellent and complete of all inspired books which brings unambiguous guidance. Orthodox Islamic teaching is that after Muhammad there can be no further prophet. The title often used for him is 'The Seal of the Prophets'. This implies not only that the message that he brought perfects the message of earlier prophets, but also that the Qur'an confirms their message as being authentic revelations from God. This being the case it is claimed that as the Qur'an is God's perfect revelation, it is a yardstick to judge the earlier scriptures in their present form. A Muslim scholar has summarized it this way, 'Those teachings which are consistent with and verified by the teachings of the Qur'an are accepted by Muslims, while those contradicting the Qur'an are believed by Muslims to be men's ideas and conceptions.'

The Qur'an stresses that Muhammad was a mortal man with no supernatural qualities. He is credited with no special knowledge beyond that which had been revealed to him nor with any power to create miracles. Nevertheless, as will be explained in a later chapter, Muhammad's life and his personal qualities are seen by Muslims as a shining example of proper humanity.

In summary: by the term prophet, Muslims understand a completely human but obedient man commissioned by God to speak his message. It is the teaching of Islam that, from the beginning of time, God has sent His prophets to different people at different times teaching of the oneness of God, and that Muhammad is God's final messenger, 'The Seal of the Prophets', who perfects and confirms the message of all the prophets who came before him.

Chapter 2

The Arabian Setting

Muslims do not think of Islam as a new religion which began with the Prophet Muhammad but believe that it is the true and original religion of mankind and that it began with the first man, Adam. According to Muslim belief, Adam was a Muslim, as were Abraham, Moses, David and Jesus, in that they all submitted to God in faith and obedience. However, in its present form, Islam is based on the career of the Prophet Muhammad, and on the revelations which he claimed to have received from God.

The first step in this book will be to look briefly at Arabia in the time of Muhammad, the country in which he was born and in which his career took place, and the Arab people of whom he was one and to whom he came to believe that he was sent. Knowing something about this background should enable a better appreciation of the significance of the revelations and of what Muhammad achieved in setting up the Community of believers.

The Land and the People

As can be seen from a map of the Middle East, Arabia is on a large peninsula bounded by the mountains of modern-day Turkey to the north, the mountains of present-day Iraq in the north east, the Indian Ocean in the south east and the Red Sea in the south west. The country, then as now, was arid, mostly desert and semi-desert. In the time of Muhammad, a large proportion of the population were nomadic Bedouin tribes-people. Their way of life was based on stock breeding and, occasionally, banditry. Each of the tribes was independent and self-ruling and there was often fierce rivalry between them. Feuding and fighting were common. The harshness of desert life and the dangers from other tribes made each individual very dependent on his own. There was scant regard for life outside of the tribe and in this situation a people's safety depended very much on the strength of their tribe and its readiness and ability to avenge any insult or injury to any of its members. If a member was killed, it was regarded as a matter of honour for the whole tribe to avenge the death by killing a member of the killer's tribe. The survival of every tribe, in turn, depended on the willingness of each of its members to fulfil this obligation.

Not all the inhabitants of Arabia were nomads at this time. There were people who lived a settled existence in oases and towns and who made their living mainly from trade and agriculture. The Bedouin were to some extent dependent on these settled areas. By their custom, raiding them and their trade caravans was not regarded as a crime and such raids were not uncommon. Often townspeople and traders were prepared to pay Bedouin tribes in return for security from these raids. There were other ties too between town dwellers and nomads. Many of the town dwellers were themselves descendants and relatives of nomads and they shared many of their customs and values. Very often the Bedouin were hired as guides and camel drivers for the trade caravans of the town dwellers.

The two largest settled areas in Central Arabia were Yathrib, later named Medina, and Mecca. Yathrib was a large oasis and its prosperity was based mainly on agriculture. Mecca was a city which existed largely on trade. It stood near the crossroads of the two major trade routes across Arabia, the routes from Yemen to Syria and from Ethiopia to Iraq. Another vital factor which had helped its growth was that it contained the Kaaba. This was an ancient stone cubical structure, which had become a major centre for pilgrimage, attracting people from all over Arabia.

By Muhammad's time, at least a section of the Meccan population had become so wealthy on the basis of this trade and pilgrimage that they owned the caravans that carried the goods. They also controlled the trade route from Yemen to Syria. The most wealthy and influential tribe in Mecca were the Quraysh. They had control of the Kaaba and owned the majority of the caravans. As has been mentioned, successful traders needed the help of Bedouin in large numbers as escorts, guides and camel drivers. They also needed the protection the Bedouin could give and the safe passage and the use of wells that they could grant. Consequently, the Quraysh used to pay the Bedouin chiefs to secure these benefits. Between the Quraysh and Bedouin tribes a system of alliances, often strengthened by ties of marriage, had grown up and it was this confederation that gave the Quraysh their power and influence. Though they themselves did not possess overwhelming military might, they could always raise a large number of allies, strong enough to subdue any rival. As will be seen, Muhammad's principal opponents were from this powerful tribe. The story of how he overcame them, and then won them over to the religion he was proclaiming, will be important in the first part of this book.

The Religious Background

In Arabia, when Muhammad's prophetic career began, there were three main religious groups: pagans, the name usually given to those who followed the traditional religion of Arabia, Jews and Christians. The main source of information about the religious situation at that time is the Qur'an itself, the book which contains a compilation of the revelations that Muhammad claimed to have received from God. The passages it contains make frequent references to these three groups, and to understand the significance of Qur'anic teaching it is necessary to know a bit about each of them, starting with the pagans.

The traditional religion of Arabia was animistic in nature. Each area had its own demon or spirit which could have its dwelling in physical objects such as trees, stones and wells. Each object made sacred by the presence of a spirit would be surrounded by an area of sanctuary within which no tree could be felled nor from which any animal could be taken. At these places, it was believed, the divinity could be contacted by the worshipper smearing the blood of a sacrifice onto the sacred object. Another common method of establishing a bond with the supernatural being was for the worshipper to walk round the sacred object. The Kaaba was the most important sanctuary in Arabia and at the time of Muhammad was home to many of the objects and statues that represented the supposedly supernatural beings.

In traditional Arabian religious belief, there were some deities who were thought to have a more definite personal nature. The Qur'an mentions three of them, Manat, al-Lat, and al-Uzza. These three were goddesses who had a large number of followers in Mecca. There is evidence from the Qur'an that when Muhammad began to preach there, he was put under pressure from the Quraysh to give them a place beside Allah, the high God, as worthy of worship.

When Muhammad started to teach his religious message in Mecca it was this God, Allah, that he proclaimed as the one and only. In so doing he was not introducing a new god. Indeed, the name Allah was to be found in pre-Islamic times in inscriptions and names. The impression given by the Qur'an is that its message is addressed to people who believed in the existence of a supreme God, though in a vague and confused way. When Muhammad proclaimed his message about Allah, it was not to tell them that He existed, but to accuse them of knowing about the supreme God and yet not worshipping Him alone, preferring to worship idols.

There had been significant numbers of Jews in Arabia since at least the destruction of Jerusalem and the dispersal of many of its people in 70 c.e. In neighbouring Yemen there had been a large Jewish colony since the fourth century c.e. By the time of Muhammad, Jewish tribes played a very significant part in the economy of Central Arabia. They owned some of the best land in the major oases and formed at least half the population of Yathrib, having made many proselytes among the Arabs there.

Christianity had come to Arabia as early as the time of St. Paul in the first century, and by the time of Muhammad there were Christian communities scattered throughout the Peninsula. Two tribes in Central Arabia had converted to Christianity and Christian monks and holy men were a common sight. The presence of significant numbers of Christians and Jews meant that their religious ideas were not unknown in Arabia and it is perhaps for this reason that the idea of one supreme God was becoming more widely known.

The powers which surrounded Arabia, the Persian and Byzantine Empires and the Kingdom of Abyssinia, were either Christian or had substantial Christian minorities. Some nomadic tribes on the borders of Arabia were gradually becoming Christianized, but this often meant becoming involved in disputes between different divisions of the Christian Church.

Chapter 3

The Early Life of Muhammad

The purpose of this chapter is to begin a study of the life and prophetic career of Muhammad in order to enable an understanding of the Community he founded and an appreciation of the Qur'an and its message.

From the writings of early Muslim historians, the facts about Muhammad's early life that are generally accepted as historical are as follows. Muhammad's paternal grandfather was Abbas ibn Abd al-Muttalib, a man of some importance in Mecca and himself a great-grandson of the founder of the city. He belonged to the clan of Hashim, part of the Quraysh tribe. One of his sons was Abu Talib, a man respected as clan leader but who had fallen on hard times. Another of his sons was a trader by the name of Abdullah, who married a woman called Amina bint Wahb, also a member of the Quraysh tribe. It was to this couple in about 570 c.e. that Muhammad was born. Before his birth however Abdullah died on a trading trip and Muhammad was put under the care of Abd al-Muttalib.

When Muhammad was six years old his mother died, leaving Muhammad an orphan, and two years later so did his grandfather and protector, leaving him in the care of his uncle, Abu Talib. Though Abu Talib himself was never to become a Muslim, throughout his life, as head of the clan, he offered Muhammad his protection against very powerful enemies. When Muhammad was twelve years old, he went on a trading trip to Syria with his uncle. As a young man he played a minor part in fighting at his uncle's side in an inter-tribal war. Concerned with injustices and inequalities in Mecca he joined an association called the *Hilf ul-Fudul,* the League of the

Just, the aims of which were to protect the defenseless and the stranger in the city from the malpractices of some of the rich.

Perhaps the most important event of Muhammad's early life was his marriage to Khadijah bint Khuwaylid, a wealthy woman who had been twice widowed. The traditional account is that when she heard of the honesty of Muhammad (his nickname was *al-amin,* the trustworthy) and of his ability, she invited him to act as her agent on a caravan journey to Syria. It goes on to state that, so impressed was she with Muhammad, though she was forty years old and he was twenty-five, she proposed marriage to him and he accepted.

Marriage to Khadijah made Muhammad a wealthy man, and though very little is known about the next fifteen or so years of his life, it appears that he took little part in business. Instead, he increasingly became drawn to a life of spiritual searching and meditation. It has been suggested that, unhappy with the social injustices and idol worship in the city, he was seeking a religious answer to these problems. Tradition tells that he came to desire solitude and made it a habit to go to a cave on Mount Hira, one of the quiet desert hills near Mecca. It was there, one night in the year 610 that he was to have an experience which changed his life, and indeed the course of world history.

The Night of Power

That night, as he meditated on his own in the desert, he began to experience vivid visions. One such vision is described in Sura 53:1-11. In this vision a 'Glorious Being' came near and revealed a message to him. According to another account, outside the Qur'an but coming from one of Muhammad's early biographers, ibn Ishaq ibn Yasin (d.

'768) and accepted throughout the Muslim world, one night as he lay sleeping the Angel Gabriel came to him with a silk cloth on which words were written. The Angel ordered him to recite these words, which were as follows:

> Proclaim! in the name of your Lord and Cherisher who created, created man out of a (mere) clot of congealed blood. Proclaim! And your Lord is Most Bountiful, He who taught (the use of) the Pen, taught man that which he knew not.

These words are to be found in Sura 96:1-5. The occasion of this, the first of all the revelations, is known as the 'Night of Power'. From this time on, until his death twenty-two years later, Muhammad received what he believed were revelations from God and which, collected together, form the Qur'an.

There is evidence though that initially the idea that he was being called by God did not come easily to Muhammad and that he went through a period of doubt and bewilderment. At first, he thought that perhaps he had been possessed by one of the *jinn* or spirits. However, he received strong support from his wife and from a cousin of hers, a Christian monk called Waraqa ibn Nawfal, who encouraged him to believe that the revelations were genuinely from God. Later in his life, especially when he faced opposition and abuse, the 'Night of Power' and other early vivid visions helped to confirm to Muhammad that he was indeed God's messenger.

The Revelations

Over twenty-two years Muhammad continued to proclaim revelations. Not many of them seem to have been accompanied by visions when Muhammad experienced them. Some passages of the Qur'an mention God sending a messenger to Muhammad. Ibn Sa'd (d. 845), one of Muhammad's early biographers, quotes him as saying,

Sometimes Gabriel visits me and tells it to me as though one man were speaking to another. He also reports Muhammad as saying that revelations came to him with the pain of a bell being rung too close to his ears. There is other evidence which suggests that the coming of a revelation was accompanied by physical symptoms. It is reported that even on cold days he would drip with sweat when he felt that a revelation was coming upon him.

As to the source of these revelations, Muslims are certain that they were totally from God. It is believed that Muhammad had no part at all in influencing what they contained. As will be shown in later chapters, Muhammad's opponents, were not so convinced, and some accused him of consciously making up the revelations to further his own ambitions.

Chapter 4

Proclaiming the Message

Muhammad did not keep the revelations to himself but communicated them first to his wife Khadijah and then to some of his closest friends, who became convinced that they were genuine. In 613 he began to proclaim his message publicly to the people of Mecca. Though there is very little indication in the Qur'an about either at what time or in what order the messages were given, by examining those passages which are generally agreed to be the earliest, it is possible to obtain an idea of the dramatic message that Muhammad proclaimed to the people of Mecca.

The message of the Qur'an will be set out in detail in chapters 9-11 of this book, but at this point the earliest themes will be summarized. The first and most important note in Muhammad's early teaching was the proclamation of the goodness and the power of God. It proclaimed that God is the maker of the universe, who miraculously created humankind and provides for their needs. The second theme was that people should realize their dependence on God and should demonstrate their gratitude to Him for His goodness by showing generosity to the destitute. The third theme was that all people will face a judgement for their deeds, a judgement that even the dead will not escape but be brought back to face.

Early Reaction in Mecca

One of the early historians of Muhammad's life gives the following account of the opening of his career.

> The messenger of God summoned to Islam secretly and openly and there responded to God whom He would of the young men and weak people so that those who believed in Him were many and the unbelieving Quraysh did not criticize what he said. (Al-Zuhri, d. 713).

There is evidence that Muhammad was careful in his first year of public preaching to keep in favour with the powerful tribe that led Meccan society. In fact, Sura 80:1-10 seems to accuse him of favouring them at the cost of neglecting the poorer and humbler people who had come to join him. However good relations with the Quraysh did not last. Al-Zuhri continued:

> This lasted until God spoke shamefully of the idols that they worshipped other than Himself and mentioned the perdition of their fathers who had died in unbelief. At that time, they came to hate the messenger of God and to be hostile to him.

From this time on Muhammad was faced with hostility and eventually persecution from the most influential section of Meccan society.

Opposition in Mecca

Because Muhammad had the protection of his clan under his uncle Abu Talib, he himself was fairly safe from physical mistreatment, so opposition to him in the early stages was mostly verbal. Many passages in the Qur'an refer to these attacks and provide answers to them. One form of attack on Muhammad was criticism of his message. The Quraysh used to make fun of his teaching that on the last day God would resurrect the bodies of the dead for judgement. There is a record of a man coming to Muhammad with a decayed human bone and asking how it could be brought back to life. Sura 45:25 reports someone saying to Muhammad, *Bring (back) our forefathers, if what you say is true!* The answer of the Qur'an was to point out the miraculous way in which children are conceived and born and to ask if raising the dead would be any more wonderful.

When Muhammad preached against their worship of idols the Quraysh did not take this so lightly but defended them with a fierce loyalty, saying that they were following the practices of their forefathers. They were infuriated, according to al-Zuhri, when Muhammad told them that their ancestors were in Hell for their practices.

As well as attacking his message, the people who opposed Muhammad also attacked his claim to be a prophet. He was frequently accused of not receiving his messages from God but being possessed by the *jinn*, evil spirits. He was also accused of making up what he claimed were revelations, or having them made up for him by someone else. Some of his opponents suggested that Muhammad could not be a prophet because he was not a person of enough importance. They argued that if God had indeed sent a messenger, He would have chosen one of the leading men of the city and not a man of little consequence like Muhammad.

For the Quraysh, Muhammad's claim to be God's messenger presented a serious political threat to their position in Mecca. By Arab tradition, the right to lead should belong to the person with the most wisdom and best judgement. If the people of the city were to accept Muhammad as God's prophet and to turn to him for guidance, this would weaken their status as the city's accepted leaders. This was one of the main reasons why they were so anxious to discredit Muhammad's claims to be God's prophet and felt increasingly threatened as he attracted followers in the city.

There was also an economic reason for the opposition from the leaders of the Quraysh. Being the hereditary guardians of the Kaaba, they drew great wealth from the pilgrims who visited it to worship the idols there and to trade in the city. Muhammad's teaching that idols should be destroyed so that God alone should be worshipped was a major threat to an important source of their prosperity.

Persecution

Although Muhammad and some of his followers were protected by their own clans from threats to their personal safety, a number of poorer and weaker people without such protection were physically mistreated. So severe was this persecution that in 615 Muhammad gave permission to some of his followers to flee to the Christian Kingdom of Abyssinia, present day Ethiopia, where they would be safe. The following year Muhammad's opponents tried to force his clan, the clan of Hashim, to give up their protection of him. Organized by Abu-Jahl a leading Qurayshite, to put further pressure on them to abandon Muhammad, the clan of Hashim was boycotted by the rest of the city. This meant that no one would have business dealings nor intermarry with them. This boycott however did not succeed and by 619 it had ended.

That same year though brought a double tragedy to Muhammad. First his wife Khadijah then his uncle Abu-Talib died. The death of his main supporter and of the man who had so long been his protector were heavy blows to Muhammad, especially because Abu Talib's successor as head of the clan, Abu Lahab, another of his uncles, eventually refused to give Muhammad the clan's protection.

Having failed to gain much support in Mecca Muhammad went to Ta'if, a town sixty miles to the east, where he preached in the hope of making converts. However, there he was met with mockery and insult and driven out of town. When he returned to Mecca his position was by that time so weak that, before he could re-enter the city, he had to negotiate for some measure of protection from one of its clan leaders.

Chapter 5

Muhammad in Medina

The Hijrah

Though the opposition of the Quraysh made it difficult for Muhammad to increase the number of his followers in Mecca, another opportunity opened up for him. In 620 six men from Yathrib heard Muhammad preach in Mecca and were convinced by what he taught. In the following two years first twelve and then seventy-five people from Yathrib came to Mecca and agreed to accept Muhammad as God's prophet. In 622 these converts invited Muhammad to move to their city. Muhammad directed his followers to leave Mecca in secret for Yathrib and a few days later he himself travelled there by a roundabout route to avoid his enemies who were, by this time, seeking to assassinate him.

This flight, or emigration of the Prophet and his followers from Mecca to Medina, as Yathrib came to be known, is called in Arabic the *hijrah*. This was a most significant event. It marked not only Muhammad's break with the city of his birth but also, more importantly, the beginning of the Islamic Community, which the Prophet came to establish in Medina. So significant was this event that Muslims have come to reckon the start of their calendar from it. While much of the world measures its dates c.e. (common era) or a.d. (a*nno domini*, from the year of our Lord), the Islamic calendar calculates its dates a.h. (a*nno hegirae*, from the year of the *hijrah*).

In Medina the political situation was much more favourable for Muhammad than it had been in Mecca. In Mecca the city had its undisputed masters, the Quraysh, who had come to oppose Muhammad because his claim to be God's Prophet was a threat to their political authority. In Medina however no one group was in control. There were two Arab tribes who were bitter rivals and had in 617 fought a bloody civil war. Though a truce had been declared, feuding still continued. What was needed in Medina was someone independent from the hostile factions who might be able to arbitrate between them. A figure who claimed to be God's Messenger might have the sort of authority that would be accepted. Muhammad came to Medina on the terms that he would be accepted as a prophet and that he would have the authority to arbitrate between the opposing factions there. This gave him a position of considerable influence in that city without making him, initially at least, its undisputed leader.

Establishing the Community of Islam

One of Muhammad's earliest actions in Medina was to build a mosque, in Arabic *masjid* (literally, a place of prostration) as a place for prayer and meeting. Once he had settled in Medina, he set about fulfilling the aim of establishing a united Community under his leader as God's spokesman. However, in spite of his position of influence he still faced considerable difficulties. For one thing, the population of the city was very divided. In addition to the feuding Arab tribes there were also three major wealthy Jewish tribes in Medina and, beyond that, his own followers from Mecca, the emigrants or *Muhajirun*. In this situation Muhammad attempted to unite all these groups into one Community by means of a Charter, or Constitution. The historian Muhammad ibn Ishaq (d. 767) records a document which contains its terms.

The document, known as the Charter of Medina, stated that all the believers from Mecca and those from Medina who had joined them and fought with them were to constitute one Community, in Arabic *Umma*, separate from others. It stated that the brotherhood of Islam should take priority over all other relationships. In other words, the bond between fellow believers was to be stronger than that of family and kinship, even more binding than that between father and son. The individuals who professed Muhammad as God's Prophet agreed, by the terms of this charter, to be united in attack and defence with all others who were party to it. In return each individual was to be given the protection of the whole Community. This meant that for those who accepted Muhammad as God's Prophet, it was the *Umma*, and no longer their tribe, to whom they owed their deepest loyalty.

It is important to note, that from this early time Islam has been more than a set of religious beliefs. It has been and is, ideally, a way of life in which legal, social, political, and economic as well as religious beliefs and practices are regulated. It is also important to recognize that belief in the unity and equality of all believers is fundamental to Islam. To this day Muslims regard Islam as a universal religion, a religion for all regardless of tribe, nation or race. The only criterion for membership of this brotherhood is acceptance that there is one God and that Muhammad is His Messenger. Muhammad's time in Medina was extremely important as it was there that he began to establish the religious and political organization that was, within a few centuries, to rule from the shores of the Atlantic to the borders of India.

Muhammad and the Jewish tribes

In the Charter of Medina some Jewish tribes were mentioned as part of the Community, without any requirement that they give up their faith. Indeed, Muhammad saw a great deal of continuity between the religions. One strand of the teaching of the Qur'an is that each people had their own prophets and that Muhammad was the prophet who had been sent by God to the Arabs. It may be that at first Muhammad believed that, as long as the Jewish tribes lived by their faith, there need be no conflict between Jews and Muslims. In his early years at Medina Muhammad instructed Muslims to face Jerusalem when they prayed and to observe the Jewish Feast of Atonement.

However, the Jewish tribes in Medina were not to be won over. They soon concluded that though Muhammad might believe that there was little difference between the message he pronounced and that of the Jewish Scriptures, in this he was mistaken. They did not take long to come to the opinion that Muhammad's knowledge of their scriptures was very deficient. Wherever the words of the Qur'an differed from those of their Bible, some were quick to point this out and pour scorn on what they claimed was his misunderstanding and misinterpretation of it.

This, naturally, posed a serious threat to Muhammad's whole position in Medina. When Jews in the city used their knowledge of their own scriptures to challenge Muhammad's claim that the Qur'an was the speech of God, they were effectively challenging his right to call himself God's Prophet. If the Qur'an was mistaken about the Jewish scriptures, then it could not be the actual words of God and Muhammad could then not be His Prophet. As Muhammad's whole position of power and influence depended on his being accepted as God's Prophet, unless he had been able to answer these charges, his whole status in Medina would have been seriously threatened.

Muhammad countered this threat in the following ways. Firstly, he made a religious break with his Jewish opponents. He proclaimed a revelation which commanded Muslims to face the Kaaba in Mecca, and not Jerusalem when they prayed. He further confirmed the break by ceasing to observe the Feast of Atonement. Next, in order to counter the charge that he had misinterpreted and misunderstood the Jewish scriptures, he declared that, where the Qur'an and their Bible did not agree, it was Jewish scripture and not the Qur'an which was in error.

At this time Muhammad's teaching and the Qur'an came to lay great stress on the figure of Abraham. They both emphasized that Islam was the religion of Abraham who, though he was neither a Jew or a Christian himself, was revered by both Jews and Christians. The religion of Abraham, Muhammad preached, was the true religion pure and simple. This religion, he proclaimed, had been the religion of all their prophets, and if Jews and Christians had different ideas and practices, it was they themselves who had created them.

In emphasizing the centrality of Abraham, Muhammad was able to claim that Islam was in no way dependent on Judaism and Christianity. He was able to portray the religion he was proclaiming not as something that came after Judaism and Christianity and was dependent on them in any way, but as the true and original religion of which Judaism and Christianity were in fact corruptions. Though this answer did not convince the Jews of Medina he was, importantly, able to convince his own followers and thus was able to keep his authority intact in their eyes.

Chapter 6

Conflict with the Quraysh

Uniting the various groups in Medina into one Islamic Community and answering challenges from the Jews in the city were not Muhammad's only problems. He also had to provide for himself and his Meccan immigrants there. To do this he turned to the age-old Arab tradition of raiding. With some of his followers he began to mount attacks on trade caravans owned by the Quraysh. At first, he met with little success but in his second year in Medina twelve of his men did manage to capture a small Meccan caravan. This provoked a wide outcry because the raid had taken place in a sacred month when, by Arab tradition, all fighting was prohibited. Muhammad's answer was that doing something that would help to bring an end to idol worship was more important than fearing to break pagan taboos.

The Battle of Badr

Six weeks after this raid Muhammad enjoyed his first military success. Having got news of a thousand camel Meccan caravan which was to pass near Medina, he went out with a mixed group of his own Meccan immigrants and Medinan helpers to intercept it. The Meccans got to hear of this and sent out a force of 950 men to defend their caravan. In the end the caravan eluded Muhammad's men but the two armies met at a well called Badr, eleven miles from Medina. The details of the battle that followed are not very clear but it is recorded that, by the end of it, Muhammad and his force had routed the much larger army of the Meccans, killing or capturing over one hundred of them, for the loss of only fourteen of their own fighters.

This victory was a very significant event. Politically the defeat at Badr was a huge blow to the prestige of the Quraysh and a boost to that of Muhammad. As a result of it some of the tribes in Arabia decided to change their allegiance from Mecca to Muhammad. In religious terms too Badr came to have great significance for Muhammad and his followers. After the years of persecution and hardship the victory there, as spectacular as it was unexpected, seemed to show them that their faith had been justified. The Qur'an has various passages which explain the victory as the work of God. Muhammad took it as a sign confirming that he was indeed God's Prophet.

In Medina itself, some people who had hesitated to support Muhammad decided to join his Community wholeheartedly and he seems to have taken advantage of his increased power there to strengthen his position. One of the Jewish tribes was expelled from the city. A feud had broken out between the Muslims and this tribe and, after being besieged for fifteen days, they agreed to depart from the city leaving their arms and large portion of their wealth behind. This was shared amongst the Muslims. At this time too Muhammad further strengthened his position in Medina by binding together leading Muslims with ties of marriage. He married his nephew Ali to his daughter Fatima, while he himself married the daughter of a leading Medinan Muslim.

The Battle of Uhud

In 625 the Quraysh made a determined effort to gain revenge for their defeat at Badr and marched on Medina with three thousand men. The two armies met just outside Medina at a hill called Uhud. At first the Muslims gained the upper hand in the fighting that followed but, when they were close to winning the battle, their discipline broke and they went to take plunder. This gave the Meccans the opportunity to counter-attack and it was the Muslims who were brought to the brink of defeat, Muhammad himself being wounded. However, the Meccans, perhaps thinking that they had done enough, did not press home their advantage and withdrew towards their own city. This allowed Muhammad and his forces to return to Medina as an army and even, next day, to make a show of pursuing their enemies.

In spite of this, the defeat at Uhud was a severe setback. People in Medina who still had not supported Muhammad asked how God could have allowed Muhammad to be wounded and his army defeated if he really was His Prophet. From this time people in Medina who did not give their support to Muhammad were referred to in the Qur'an as 'Hypocrites'. Muhammad had interpreted victory at Badr as a sign of God's favour. After the battle of Uhud he proclaimed a further revelation that explained the defeat. Sura 3:140-148 suggested that God had allowed the Muslims to suffer in order to test their faithfulness and to see if they were indeed true believers.

Expansion and Consolidation

In the two years after the battle of Uhud Muhammad continued working to spread the message of Islam and bring more Bedouin tribes under his influence. He had some successes but also some setbacks, as when forty Qur'an reciters whom he had sent out as missionaries were massacred. This lowered the morale of his supporters. However, their spirits were lifted when they got to share the weapons and land of a second Jewish tribe whom Muhammad expelled from the city on the suspicion that they had plotted against his life.

As a result of the warlike times many Muslim men had died leaving widows and orphans. During this period Muhammad proclaimed several revelations which led to a reform of the marriage system. One such revelation is found in Sura 4:3a.

> If you fear that you shall not be able to deal justly with the orphans, marry women of your choice, two, three, four; but if you fear you shall not be able to deal justly (with them), then only one.

This passage is the basis for the toleration that Islam has for the marriage of up to four wives. The context shows that it was designed primarily to make sure that widows and orphans should be provided for.

In 627 the Meccans, under the Quraysh, made a final effort to defeat Muhammad. They managed to amass a force of ten thousand of their own citizens and Bedouin allies and marched on Medina. They negotiated with the remaining major Jewish tribe in Medina to attack Muhammad's forces from inside the city. However, Muhammad was able to outmanoeuvre his enemies. He had a large trench dug round the city which prevented a cavalry attack. Unable to enter, the Meccans were forced to sit in the surrounding desert and try to besiege the city. Muhammad was then able to divide and confuse the Meccans and their allies through a combination of bribery, trickery and skilful diplomacy so that the attacking force eventually broke up and left, having accomplished nothing.

Immediately Muhammad turned on the Jewish tribe who had plotted against him. He besieged their strongholds and forced them to surrender unconditionally. The decision as to what was to be done with them was given to one of Muhammad's most zealous supporters, a man who had suffered wounds in the fighting. His verdict was that their seven hundred men should be executed and the women and children sold as slaves.

Significantly, Medinan Muslims who had strong ties with this Jewish tribe did nothing to stop this happening, showing how, in that city, the rule of Islam had taken over from the old traditions and alliances as the standard by which people ordered their actions.

Chapter 7

Muhammad Wins Mecca

The failure of the Meccans to crush Muhammad at the siege of Medina made it clear that they could no longer hope to defeat him. From this time on Muhammad did not have to worry about survival but was able to concentrate on plans to win over all of Arabia.

The Treaty of al-Hudaybiyyah

Muhammad pursued a policy of making alliances with the tribes which were friendly to him and raiding those who opposed him. He made his first move toward winning control of Mecca when, in 628, he set out with one thousand unarmed men on a pilgrimage to the Kaaba. When the Meccans heard this, they sent out forces to block his way. After tense days of negotiations, a treaty, named after the place where the two sides met, al-Hudaybiyyah, was drawn up.

By the terms of this treaty the Muslims were not to make their pilgrimage at that time but would be allowed into Mecca on pilgrimage the following year. It was also agreed that there was to be a ten-year truce between the Meccans and Muslims and that Bedouin tribes were to be free to make treaties with either the Meccans or Muhammad as they wished. This last clause turned out to be most significant. So many tribes did switch allegiance from Mecca to Muhammad that Abu Bakr, Muhammad's oldest friend and his successor, is reported to have said that no victory brought so many followers to Islam as did the treaty of al-Hudaybiyyah.

In 629, in accordance with the terms of the treaty, Muhammad entered Mecca as a pilgrim with two thousand of his followers. The men of Mecca withdrew from the city to avoid any clashes. While he was there, Muhammad contracted another marriage, this time to a Meccan woman who was the sister-in-law of his own clan leader. This was an act of reconciliation with the clan which had once disowned him. This policy of seeking reconciliation with his enemies, rather than revenge against them, can also be seen in what Muhammad did when he finally took control of Mecca.

The Capture of Mecca

Muhammad's opportunity to move to take over the city came when a tribe allied to the Meccans made an attack on a tribe allied to Muhammad. Despite an attempt by the leaders of the Quraysh to smooth over the incident, Muhammad chose to regard it as a breach of the treaty of al-Hudaybiyyah. When the allied tribe appealed to Muhammad for help, he gathered a force of ten thousand men and marched on Mecca. Muhammad had judged, correctly, that his army would be large enough to overawe his opponents into submission. As he approached Mecca its leader, Abu-Sufyan ibn Harb, came out to meet him and handed over the city. It was agreed that everyone who stayed indoors would be safe and on the Eleventh of January 630 Muhammad entered Mecca.

One of his first acts was to go to the Kaaba. He asked for, and was given, the keys to the sanctuary and had the idols there, inside and out, destroyed. Then from the door of the Kaaba he declared that the days of paganism were over and that all the privileges, debts, blood guilt and other obligations of the pagan era were at an end.

Though it was the Meccans, and the Quraysh in particular, who had been his bitterest opponents and had tried to kill him, Muhammad showed great magnanimity and generosity toward them in their defeat. What he wanted was control of the city and not its destruction. Mecca was the strategic centre of all of Arabia and to be its master would give Muhammad greatly increased power and influence. In addition, it contained men of great military and administrative ability who would be very helpful to him in establishing the Muslim empire that he already envisaged. He therefore spared no effort to win over those who had led the opposition to him. He was in fact so generous to these people that some of his oldest and most faithful followers complained that, when they campaigned together, all the best booty was being given to the most recent converts. Muhammad answered them by saying that this was necessary to win over their hearts.

Within a few months Muhammad had been so successful in reconciling with the Meccans that they were fighting side by side with him against an army of nomadic tribesmen. This engagement, at a place called Hunayn, marked the end of any significant opposition to Muhammad in Arabia. By 632 almost all of the tribes of the Peninsula had joined Muhammad's confederation, either by agreement or because of military pressure.

Muhammad's Final Years

In 631 Muhammad led a large force of Muslims on an expedition to the north west of Arabia, perhaps as a move against the Byzantine Empire, or as a show of force for the tribes of that area. As a result of this campaign several Christian princes there decided to come under the control and protection of the Muslim confederation. Under Muhammad, Jews and Christians, the 'People of the

Book', who did this were not required to give up their religion though they did have to pay a special tax, the *jizya,* for this status.

In 632 Muhammad made a pilgrimage to Mecca for the last time. What he did there on that occasion is to this day emulated by Muslims when they themselves perform their obligatory pilgrimage. While in Mecca he is reported to have given his last sermon summarizing the duties of Muslims. On his return to Medina, it was clear that he was seriously ill. He commanded Abu Bakr to replace him as the leader of prayer at the mosque and asked permission from the rest of his wives to leave off visiting them in turn so that he could remain with his favourite, Aisha. On the eighth of June 632 he attended the mosque for prayer but that night he died. He was buried the following day.

Muhammad's Legacy

Muhammad was always careful to stress that he was in no way superhuman. He did not claim to be a wonder worker. However, throughout history Muslims have held Muhammad in the highest regard. In a previous chapter it was explained how Muhammad is regarded as 'The Seal of the Prophets', God's last messenger who brought His definitive word to humankind. As will be explained, when Muhammad died, he was succeeded as leader of the community by a line of Caliphs. However, these men did not take his place as God's spokesman.

As well as being revered as the one to whom the Qur'an was given Muhammad has been, and is, regarded by Muslims as an ideal example. This idea has its basis in the Qur'an itself where Sura 33:21 reports God as saying, *You have indeed in the Messenger of Allah a beautiful pattern (of conduct) for anyone whose hope is in Allah and the Final Day, and who engages much in the praise of Allah.*

The first source of guidance in the way of Islam, or *Shariah,* is the Qur'an itself. The Qur'an however does not provide guidance for every situation in life. Where this is the case, the Muslim Community has turned to the example of the Prophet and his sayings that were not divinely inspired. As will be explained more fully later, the accounts of what Muhammad said and did, as distinct from the words which are believed to be divinely inspired, are known collectively as the *Hadith*. The way of the Prophet's life that is contained in the *Hadith* is known as the *Sunna*. and it is this which provides the second basis of the *Shariah*. Even the smallest points of Muhammad's life have come have great significance. The great Muslim scholar al-Ghazali wrote in the eleventh century,

> Know that the key of happiness is following the Sunna and imitating the Apostle in all his goings out and comings in, his movements and times of quiescence, even in the manner of his eating, his deportment and his speech.

Books written by Muslims about Muhammad tend to deal with him in a very reverential way, praising his excellent character and noble manners, his wisdom, bravery, generosity, mercy and other good qualities. This reverence for Muhammad makes it most unusual for any books written about him by Muslims to contain any harsh judgements of him. Muslims can react in a hostile way to any denigration of him. Despite this high regard for their Prophet, Muslims firmly reject being called 'Muhammadans' as this might suggest that they worship Muhammad when it is God alone who is worthy of this.

THE FOUNDATIONS OF ISLAM

Part 2: The Book

Chapter 8

The Qur'an

From what has been written in previous chapters it is clear Muhammad proclaimed sections of the Qur'an at particular times, in particular places and, in some cases, in response to particular circumstances. The message of the Book cannot be completely understood without reference to this historical background. It must also be appreciated, however, that Muslims believe that the message of the Qur'an applies to all times, in all places and to all people. For Muslims the Qur'an is literally 'The Word of God'. Unlike most Christians and Jews who recognize a human, as well as a divine element, in the writing of their Bibles, Muslims regard the Qur'an as entirely God's creation. The belief that every word of the Qur'an comes from God is expressed in the Muslim doctrine that the Qur'an they have is an exact copy of the Eternal Qur'an which has existed for all time in Heaven.

Because the Qur'an is regarded by them as the very words of God, Muslims throughout the world put great importance on being able to read its sounds in the original Arabic. Children are ideally expected to learn to read it and recite passages by heart. Learning to recite the sacred sounds often takes priority over being able to translate their meaning. The Qur'an has been translated into very many languages but generally Muslims do not regard the resulting books as the Qur'an proper. It is believed that it cannot be translated without losing some of its force and meaning. Because for them it contains the Word of God, Muslims generally treat copies of the Qur'an with the greatest respect. Muslims are required to do the ritual washing before opening a Qur'an. Some believe that only a Muslim may handle it. Among Muslims words from the Qur'an are part of everyday life and events of any importance, such as eating, travel and business transactions, can be accompanied by the recitation of an appropriate passage.

The Divisions of the Qur'an

The Qur'an is divided into 114 chapters or *Surat* (singular *Sura*) which are in turn divided into verses or *Ayat* (singular *Aya*). The first chapter known as *al-Fatiha*, the opening, is a short prayer. After this the chapters are arranged in order of length with the longest at the beginning and the shortest at the end. Because of the way the Qur'anic passages are organized there are few clues as to the circumstances in which each passage was proclaimed and it has proved impossible for scholars to be certain about the date, or even the order, of the passages. It is widely agreed though that the earlier passages, proclaimed in Mecca, tend to be shorter and to have a more marked poetical rhythm. The later Medinan passages tend to be longer and more prosaic, dealing often with guidance for the regulation of the community and accounts of the earlier prophets.

The Compilation of the Qur'an

The Muslim tradition is that Muhammad could neither read or write, making the production of the Qur'an all the more miraculous. At first the words were not written down but memorized by heart by some of his followers. By the time of Muhammad's death however most of the words had been committed to writing. There is evidence that in Medina Muhammad used secretaries who would have been able to record the words in written form. It is possible that the Prophet himself brought many of the passages together and put them into some kind of order.

There is a tradition that after Muhammad's death his secretary Zaid ibn Thabit, on the authority of Abu Bakr, Muhammad's successor as leader of the Islamic Community, collected all the Qur'anic passages from every available source, *Pieces of flat stones, palm leaves, shoulder blades and ribs of animals, pieces of papyrus, leather and wooden boards, as well as from the hearts of men.*

Whatever the accuracy of this tradition, the resulting compilation was only one of several that circulated for a time. There is evidence that the existence of several versions of the Qur'an was causing disputes within different sections of the Muslim army and when this was reported to Uthman, the third Caliph, he and the most senior of Muhammad's companions met and commissioned ibn Thabit to draw up a definitive collection of the Holy Scripture. When he had done his work, copies of the agreed text were written out and dispatched to all the major centres of Islam. Tradition adds that all other versions were burned. The date for this compilation lies between 650 and 655 and the version which resulted is the one which has survived unchanged to this day.

Chapter 9

The Teaching about God in the Qur'an

Though the Qur'an does not present its teaching systematically or thematically, its 114 chapters give a strong message about what Muslims should believe and how they should live their lives. These teachings have remained the basis of Islamic belief and practice since Muhammad established the *Umma*. The following three chapters offer a brief outline of the teaching of the Qur'an about three of its main themes: God, humankind and God's judgement.

The Unity of God

The most important theme in the teaching of the Qur'an is about God, and its central message is that God is one, God is alone, God is not divided, God has no partners nor associates. The Qur'an insists that this is the great truth that must be believed. Sura 112 states,

> Say: He is Allah, the One and Only; Allah, the Eternal, Absolute; He begets not, nor is He begotten; And there is none like unto Him.

The Qur'an condemns anything that might deny the unity of God. Pagans are condemned for worshipping idols instead of God. In Sura 9:30-32 the beliefs of Jews and Christians are also attacked for denying God's unity. In other passages such as Sura 5:73 the Christian doctrine of the Trinity is condemned for suggesting that God is one of three. The Islamic term for anything that denies the unity of God is *shirk*, and this is the major sin.

God as Creator and Sustainer

The Qur'an teaches that God is almighty, the creator and sustainer of the universe and everything in it, including all its creatures. According to the Qur'an God is all-knowing and all-seeing. A title frequently given to God is 'Lord of the Worlds'. The Qur'an frequently, as in Sura 30:20-27, claims that intelligent people can come to realize not only God's unity but also His greatness in the way that the universe has been created and humankind sustained and cared for. The Qur'an's teaching is that along with His transcendent greatness God is also close to each individual. This is illustrated in the following passages.

> Whatever is in the heavens and on earth, let it declare the Praises and Glory of Allah: for He is the Exalted in Might, the Wise. To Him belongs the dominion of the heavens and the earth: it is He Who gives Life and Death; and He has power over all things. He is the First and the Last, the Evident and the Immanent: and He has full knowledge of all things. He it is Who created the heavens and the earth in six Days, and is moreover firmly established on the Throne (of authority). He knows what enters within the earth and what comes forth out of it, what comes down from heaven and what mounts up to it. And He is with you wherever you may be. And Allah sees well all that you do. To Him belongs the dominion of the heavens and the earth: and all affairs are referred back to Allah. He merges Night into Day, and He merges Day into Night; and He has full knowledge of the secrets of (all) hearts. Sura 57:1-6.

> It was We Who created man, and We know what dark suggestions his soul makes to him: for We are nearer to him than (his) jugular vein. Sura 50:16.

The Qur'an teaches that while God is all powerful, He is also generous and merciful. Indeed, every Sura except one begins with the formula, *In the name of God, the Compassionate, the Merciful*. The message of the Qur'an is that God's generosity to humankind is shown in the way that He provides for all their needs. Evidence of God's mercy is shown by His readiness to forgive and also by the guidance He has given about how people can live the good life by sending them the prophets and the sacred books.

God's Sovereign Will

In the teaching of the Qur'an there is also another side to God's guidance and this is that God chooses who it is that will be guided. Suras 10:99 and 100 state,

> If it had been your Lord's Will they all would have believed - all who are on earth! ..... no soul can believe except by the Will of Allah.

The teaching of the Qur'an is that God's will is sovereign. There are no laws and principles which can bind it. It is beyond human understanding and cannot be called into question. So much is God in control of the world, according to the Qur'an, that everything that happens in it is foreordained by God, nothing can happen which is beyond His control. It teaches that no good or evil can happen to a person unless God wills it. Paradoxically though, as will be discussed in the following chapter, the Qur'an also teaches that people are responsible for all their actions and will have to answer for them on the Day of Judgement.

Much of the Qur'anic teaching about God can be summed up in the titles that it gives to Him. Known as 'The Beautiful Names', these include the Mighty, the Most-High, the Knowing, the Producer, the Creator, the Wise, the Just, the True and, first and foremost, the Merciful.

Chapter 10

The Teaching of the Qur'an about Humankind

People Dependent on God

What the Qur'an teaches about people cannot be meaningfully separated from what it teaches about God. The corollary of the doctrine that God is creator is that humans are His creatures, the other side of its teaching that God is the sustainer is the doctrine that people are completely dependent on Him.

Sura 16:1-18 details some of the ways in which God provides for human beings; through His guidance, through animals for the benefits they bring, through rain, through crops, through day and night, through colours, through the oceans with all they contain, and through stars and landmarks. This passage ends with the sentence, *If you would count up the favours of Allah, never would you be able to number them: for Allah is Oft-Forgiving, Most Merciful.*

As was stated in the previous chapter, the Qur'an teaches that men and women are so dependent on God's guidance that they cannot choose to follow the straight path unless God Himself wills it. Its message is that people are unable to defy God. According to the Qur'an, even people's apparent rebellion against God is a delusion. If a person does go against God's laws it is because God has foreordained it. However, in spite of this teaching of people's dependence on God and their subjection to His sovereign will, the Qur'an at the same time teaches that they are responsible for their actions and will have to answer for them on the Day of Judgement. (The Qur'an itself does not explain this paradox and, as will be shown in chapters 17 and 18, it was left to Islamic theologians of later centuries to try to resolve it.)

How People should Respond to God

The Qur'an teaches that the proper response to God is to submit and to be obedient. The book makes it clear that God is master, *raab,* and man is servant, *abd.* Indeed, the very term 'Muslim', is used in the Qur'an to signify a person who has submitted to God. Islam is of course the name given to the religion. The postures which Muslims adopt in ritual prayer, bowing and prostrating with their foreheads to the ground, express this submission to God.

The Qur'an makes it clear that another proper response to God is gratitude. Sura 39:7 illustrates how, though God is above the need for people's thanks, it still pleases Him.

> If you reject (Allah), truly Allah has no need of you; but He likes not ingratitude from his servants: if you are grateful, He is pleased with you.

The Qur'an also encourages people to put their trust in God. In Sura 13:30 believers are commanded to say,

> He is my Lord! There is no god but He! On Him is my trust, and to Him do I turn.

In doing this, the Qur'an says people will be following the examples of Noah, Jacob and Muhammad himself.

Though the Qur'an emphasizes people's lowliness before God, it gives them a very high status, that of His Caliph, or representative, over the rest of creation and emphasizes their responsibilities for their stewardship of it.

The Qur'an teaches that every individual is born innocent, free of any sin. Compare this with the Christian doctrine of original sin where every child inherits sin at birth from the disobedience of Adam. The message of the Qur'an is that every person is responsible for his or her own sins and shortcomings and that no one can carry the sins of anyone else. Consequently, the Christian doctrine that people are essentially fallen and need a Saviour to take away their guilt is very different from that of the Qur'an. Its message is that humans are weak by nature, rather than sinful, but also that God is aware of their weakness and never rejects sincere repentance. It is the Islamic belief that this idea of humans as responsible beings, able to work out the right way, through the guidance that has been given to them, gives people both freedom and dignity.

Right-doing

In the Qur'an people are called to right-doing and it spells out what duties, thoughts and actions are involved in being obedient to God. There are four basic religious duties mentioned. The first of these is performing ritual prayer or *Salat*. The duty of prayer, the ritual washing that should be done before it and when it should be performed, is mentioned in various passages. Sura 62:9 gives the command to pray on Fridays.

> O you who believe! When the call is proclaimed to prayer on Friday (the Day of Assembly), hasten earnestly to the remembrance of Allah, and leave off business (and traffic): that is best for you if you did but know it.

A second religious duty prescribed in the Qur'an is that of charitable giving, *Zakat*, which purifies the giver and wins God's favour. This command to give alms is frequently linked with the command to pray, and the Qur'an stresses that worship without generosity to the needy is empty.

A third prescribed religious duty, *Sawm*, is fasting during the month of Ramadan and guidance on what this involves is laid out in Sura 2:183-185. The fourth religious duty is making the pilgrimage, *Hajj*, to Mecca with Sura 2:196-199 setting out some guidance as to what should be done to fulfil it.

These four religious duties prayer, almsgiving, fasting and pilgrimage, along with the Profession of Faith, the *Shahada*, that there is no god except for God and that Muhammad is the Prophet of God, are so fundamental to the practice of the religion that they are known as the Five Pillars of Islam. How the regulations about each of them reached their final form will be explained in Chapter 14.

In setting out how God wishes people to behave, the Qur'an has plenty to say about family life, much of it contained in Sura 4:1-35. People should treat their parents with respect. Men should treat their wives with kindness and fairness. Women are directed to be chaste and modest. Adultery is condemned and punishments for it are set out. The Qur'an lays down laws about divorce. There are a number of regulations which prohibit the exploitation of widows and orphans and about inheritance. The killing of female babies is prohibited.

The Qur'an also gives instructions about what can and cannot be eaten. Sura 6:145 prohibits the flesh of pigs or carrion or of an animal not killed in the approved way. The Qur'an prohibits gambling and the drinking of wine. It also forbids the lending of money for interest.

The Qur'an also lays on believers the obligation of struggling for the sake of God, *jihad*. This can involve the struggle of people against the evil within themselves, the 'greater *jihad*'. For the Community of believers, it can involve, in certain circumstances, that of taking up arms, the 'lesser *jihad*.'

Chapter 11

The Teaching of the Qur'an about Judgement, Paradise and Hell

Sura 86:4 states that every soul has a watcher. Sura 43:80 tells that angels are at people's side recording all they do and say, and there are numerous references to the books into which these accounts will be written. The Qur'an repeatedly makes it clear that people are going to be called to answer for their beliefs and actions on the Day of Judgement and that an eternal reward or punishment will follow.

The Day of Judgement

The Qur'an contains many striking images which describe the awe and terror of that day. One extended passage, Sura 69:13-37, tells of a blast on a trumpet, mountains becoming dust, the sky torn asunder and angels bringing down God's throne. In His presence people will be given a book containing the record of their deeds and some will be destined for reward in Paradise and others for punishment in Hell. Other passages tell of the sun ceasing to shine and the stars falling down, of people, both living and resurrected from the dead, being gathered together in trepidation before God and having the books of their good and bad deeds weighed against each other on scales.

The Qur'an also indicates the criteria by which people will be judged. Those who have not believed in the Day of Reckoning, denied the truth of God's message and neglected to share their wealth with the needy will be condemned, while those who have believed, put aside some of their wealth for the needy, attended their prayers, kept their trusts and promises and lived virtuous lives will be rewarded. Sura 47:4-6 adds martyrs to this list of those destined for Paradise. Further categories of people facing condemnation in Hell are those who have worshipped other gods and who have not heeded the warnings in the Qur'an and from the Prophets. After judgment has been given people will be admitted to Paradise or dragged off by angels to Hell.

Paradise

In the Qur'an, through many vivid images, Paradise is pictured as a garden of ease, comfort and luxury where none of the joys of life are lacking and all of its discomforts and inconveniences, like hard work and weariness, are banished. Sura 76:5-22 is one of many passages which promises a reward for those who have been faithful, obedient, and generous to the poor. In the garden, dressed in silken robes, they will lie on soft couches, untroubled by heat or cold, with fruit in plenty and drink served by flawless youths. These images are repeated and amplified in Suras 55:46-77 and 56:8-40, which add that the blessed will be rewarded by being granted chaste paradise maidens as companions. Sura 36:56 pictures the faithful reclining on couches with their companions.

There are also passages in the Qur'an which describe the spiritual joys promised to the blessed. Sura 35:32-33 tells that in Paradise they will know God's forgiveness and that all sorrow has been removed from them. Sura 56:26 promises that the blessed will hear the words 'peace, peace', and Sura 15:47 that they will have all hatred taken from their hearts.

Hell

Though the Qur'an has less to say about Hell than about Paradise, very often passages about Paradise, the blessed and their joys there, are accompanied by descriptions of Hell, the damned and the torments that they are to suffer. Sura 76:4 speaks of the chains and fetters and the blazing fire prepared for the damned. Sura 56:41-56 adds that those who refused to believe in resurrection and judgement will be brought to a place of scorching winds, dark smoke and boiling water which they will be forced to drink. To eat they will be given disgusting food. Other passages describe the damned being showered with the boiling water and being beaten with iron rods without any possibility of escape.

THE FOUNDATIONS OF ISLAM

Part 3: Islamic Law and Guidance

Chapter 12

Regulating the Community

Christianity for its first three hundred or so years, grew and developed as a private religion in which believers were subject to the powers of the state. The early growth and spread of the Islamic Community were brought about, not by individual believers going out and propagating the faith in a non-Muslim environment, but rather by the enlargement of that Community in which, ideally, every sphere of life, social, political and economic, as well as religious was governed by Islamic principles. From its inception the Islamic Community did not separate a Muslim's duty as a believer from that as a citizen, between what was owed to God and what was owed to society.

The Charter of Medina, which Muhammad drew up to unite the different groups in the city into one *Umma*, demanded that people gave their complete allegiance to this Community, which was to take over from their tribe as the centre of their loyalties and responsibilities. Therefore, in the earliest period, to become a Muslim involved not only professing belief in the one God, but also accepting the religious and political authority of the Prophet. When Islam spread beyond Medina, it was often tribes rather than individuals who joined the Community. Tribes who allied with Muhammad had to promise to observe the religious duties of prayer and almsgiving in order to enjoy the political benefits of the alliance. So, unlike Christianity which grew and developed, at least for its first three hundred years, with its believers being subject to the authority of the existing political powers, Islam came imposing its own authority over the Community it created.

The First two Sources of Authority

The phrase 'Obey God and the Prophet' occurs forty or so times in the Qur'an, and during his lifetime, the Community of Muslims was regulated by the teachings that came from the Qur'an and the guidance of Muhammad himself. Chapter 10 in this book mentions some of the regulations contained in the Qur'an which controlled the life of the Community, such as religious duties, provisions for the poor, marriage, inheritance, divorce, usury and diet. While Muhammad was alive, where the Qur'an was silent, the Community tended to be guided by the Prophet's own example and pronouncements. There is a tradition that in his farewell sermon to his followers Muhammad told them that he was leaving with them both God's word and his own example to guide them.

The death of Muhammad in 632 brought an end both to the revelations and his own leadership of the Community. His oldest friend, Abu Bakr was chosen by Muhammad's closest companions to take his place as leader and he, and the people who succeeded him, took the title of Caliph or successor. Under the Caliphs the Qur'an continued as the first and most basic source for regulating the Community. For matters on which the Qur'an was silent, people continued to turn to what Muhammad had said and done. He indeed came to be held up as the model of what every Muslim should be like. His example, known as the *Sunna*, came to be regarded as the second source of authority, after the Qur'an, for regulating the lives of individual Muslims and the Muslim Community.

Hadith

What the Prophet had said and done was so important for the Islamic Community as it grew and developed that people thought it necessary to preserve and pass on his sayings and practices. Particularly important were the traditions of what he had said about how passages from the Qur'an should be interpreted or which had a bearing on points of law. However, his wise and instructive sayings and even seemingly trivial details of his daily habits were also recorded and kept alive. These traditions about Muhammad's words and actions tended to be passed on in the form of short stories, known as *Hadith* which were claimed to have to come from the lips of the Prophet's companions. It was through these *Hadith* that the *Sunna* of the Prophet was passed on and it was this *Sunna* that Muslims were encouraged to follow. The study of the *Hadith*, because it is the vehicle which has carried the *Sunna* of the Prophet, became a subject of great importance among Muslim scholars.

Within two or three generations of the Prophet's death very large numbers of *Hadith* had come into existence, professing to record what Muhammad had said and done and it became obvious that not all of them could be genuine. There were several reasons why *Hadith* might be manufactured. With the growth of religious sects and political parties, which will be described in chapters that follow, traditions came to be made up to justify and legitimize their own particular practices and beliefs. Furthermore, as the Islamic Community expanded to take in different countries and different religious centres emerged, each developed its own customs, and would justify them by attributing their origins to the Prophet. The method for doing this was to produce *Hadith* to prove that what they were doing Muhammad himself had done or approved of. In this manner such unrelated material as Roman legal maxims, Greek wise sayings and parables of Jesus all became attributed to Muhammad, in the form of *Hadith*.

It became obvious to the scholars who took it on themselves to build up a code of regulations to govern the life of the Islamic Community that some method was needed to check the proliferation of unsound *Hadith* and to differentiate between those which were genuine and those which were not. The method which they eventually adopted was to insist that each *Hadith* be accompanied by an account of how it had been passed on. In other words, what was required to authenticate a tradition was a chain of informants stretching back to the person who had seen the incident or heard the original saying.

During the second and third centuries after the time of the Prophet the scholars built up a science of *Hadith* criticism. In order to check the validity of the chains of informants for any tradition it was necessary for there to be much information about Muhammad's contemporaries, the 'Companions', about Muslims of the second generation, the 'Followers', and about the third generation, the 'Followers of the Followers', who they were, where they lived and whether or not they were reliable witnesses. On the basis of the strength of the chain of informants each tradition could be classified as 'sound', having no weak links, or 'weak'. The first authoritative work on this subject was by ibn Sa'd (d. 870).

The first authoritative collection of all sound traditions was made by Muhammad al-Bukhari (d. 870). It is said that he made a selection of between 3,000 to 4,000 separate 'sound' *Hadith* from around 600,000 traditions. A further collection was made by Muslim ibn al-Hajjaj (d. 875) and these two books, along with four other collections brought together in the next generation, became accepted as canonical. These *Hadith* accepted by the scholars as sound, and carrying the tradition of the Prophet, became the second source of authority on which the scholars of Islam based their rules for the regulation of the Muslim Community.

Chapter 13

The Scholars of Islam, the *Ulema*

The great motivating force in Islam has always been to do the will of God. From early on in its history the Community of Islam has had a class of learned people, known as the *Ulema,* who have made it their work to study how the will of God can be known and to translate this study into forming a practical code for Muslims to follow so that they are living in obedience to God's commands. It is because of this that there has always been a close link between Theology and Law in Islam. It was not until the second century of the Muslim era that scholars began to distinguish between the study of the two and specialize in one or the other. Theologians came to concern themselves with the doctrines and dogmas of Islam, what they called 'the roots of religion'. Jurisprudists, on the other hand, dealt with the practice of Islam, in a study known as *fiqh*. This study consisted of the formation of precepts and commands to be obeyed, rules and customs to be observed and duties to be fulfilled. These things they called 'the branches of religion'. Our concern in this and the next chapter is with these scholars, the processes that they developed to come to their judgements and the code of guidance they established on how Muslims can follow the right way, or the *Shariah*.

At first those who took an interest in drawing up a code of Islamic practice were not organized in any formal way. In the main cities and Islamic centres scholars would meet in the mosques to discuss how the Islamic Community could be guided on proper religious principles. By virtue of their ability, certain men whose opinions were highly regarded would emerge as leaders. It was they who formed the *Ulema*. It is important to note that these specialists in the practical rules of religion were generally a class distinct from the administrators, judges and officials of the Islamic state. These officials had the task of solving the practical legal problems of administering a system of law that would be effective in controlling what had become a very diverse group of peoples. The Islamic jurisprudists were concerned with working out an ideal system for the guidance of the Islamic Community that was in line with God's will. Though sometimes enjoying the encouragement of Caliphs, these pious theorists often disagreed with and condemned rulers and state officials when they felt that they were straying from the pure Islamic practice as contained in the Qur'an and *Hadith* and set out in the *Shariah*.

The Sources of Authority of Islamic Law

The jurisprudists among the *Ulema* based the code of guidance they were developing first of all on the Qur'an and then on the example of the Prophet as contained in the *Hadith*. However, it was obvious that these two sources did not contain guidance for every possible situation. According to one *Hadith* the prophet himself realized that this was the case. It reports that Muhammad once asked a judge, whom he was sending to the Yemen, on what he would base his legal decisions.

> 'On the Qur'an', was the judge's reply.
>
> 'What if you find no guidance there?' Muhammad asked.
>
> 'On the *Sunna* of the Prophet.' came the answer.
>
> 'And what if that fails you? Muhammad asked again.
>
> 'Then I shall use my own judgement.'

Muhammad is said to have approved the judge's answer.

Although the administrators of the Islamic state, the provincial governors and the judges they appointed, did give legal judgements based on their own opinions, these were not used by the *Ulema* to build up their legal code. In time, this class of scholars came to be grouped into four major Schools. Each of them developed their own particular method of arriving at a judgement when they went beyond the authority of the Qur'an and *Hadith* and each worked out their own distinctive codification of 'the practical rules of religion'.

The first of these legal Schools to codify how the duties of Islam should be carried out was that of Abu Hanifa (d. 767). This Hanifite School had its centre in Baghdad in Iraq, by that time the capital of the Islamic State. This School allowed a considerable element of personal judgement, based on common sense or 'equitable thinking', to guide their pronouncements on matters on which the Qur'an and *Hadith* were silent.

At about the same time in Medina another School of Law developed its own codification. It took its name, the Malikite School, from its leader Malik ibn Anas (d. 795). Perhaps not surprisingly, given that it was founded in Muhammad's own city, this School laid much emphasis on the practice of the Prophet in reaching their pronouncements, but also allowed judgements based on what was thought to be in the common interest.

Shortly after this the Shafi-ite School, led by Muhammad Idris ibn al-Shafii (d. 820), came to prominence in Cairo in Egypt and in Baghdad. Al-Shafii established a procedure for going beyond the Qur'an and *Hadith* that became generally accepted by Muslim jurisprudists. This procedure was known as *qiyas,* or argument by analogy. This involved basing a judgement on an issue for which the Qur'an or *Hadith* gave no direct guidance on a comparison with a similar or analogous issue for which judgement had been made on their authority. For example, the Qur'an forbids wine because it intoxicates. On this basis it was ruled that other alcoholic drinks should also be forbidden, because they too intoxicate.

The Hanbalite School was the last to be established. Taking its name from Ahmad ibn Hanbal (d. 885) it was also centred in Baghdad. His school is the most conservative of the four, basing its codification more exclusively on the Qur'an and the *Hadith*. It was suspicious of *qiyas* as a way of arriving at judgements on the grounds that it relied too much on human invention.

From about the middle of the second century of the Islamic era it came to be generally accepted that any point of practice not covered by the Qur'an or *Hadith*, but on which the learned scholars agreed, should be accepted as binding on Muslims. This consensus of the scholars has the Arabic term *ijma*. The justification for using this consensus as an authority on which Islamic law could be based came from a saying of Muhammad that God's Community would never agree on error. For this purpose, the *Ulema* were regarded as the Community's representatives.

It was on the basis of these four sources of authority, the Qur'an, the *Hadith*, *qiyas* and *ijma*, that Islamic jurisprudists worked out in detail not only the laws but also the rituals and practices which are today the distinguishing marks of Islam and the Islamic Community. As stated earlier in the chapter, this ideal code of law and guidance, drawn up on the basis of the four sources of authority is known as the *Shariah*.

To this day Sunni Muslims are identified with one of the four Schools. While there are minor differences between each of them on points of practice, these are trivial in comparison with what they have in common. Each School recognizes the others as equally orthodox.

Followers of the Schools tend to be grouped geographically. Members of the Malikite School are mostly found in North and West Africa. The Hanifite school is now the largest and predominates in the Indian subcontinent, Central Asia and Turkey. Malawi's Asian Muslims are generally Hanifite. Followers of the Shafi-ite School are mostly to be found in Southern Egypt, Syria, and East Africa. Malawian Muslims generally belong to this School. The Hanbalite School is the most conservative. Though influential, being the one that guides Saudi Arabia, it is also numerically the smallest, being confined mostly to that country.

Chapter 14

The Obligations of Islam

The Religious Obligations

Having studied the origins and development of the ideal Islamic law or *Shariah* we now turn to the duties and obligations that it enjoins on Muslims, following the practice of the Schools of Law by starting with the regulations which govern worship and religious rites and ceremonies.

Prayer

The first religious duty for Muslims is that of ritual prayer or *Salat*. While, as we have seen, this duty is mentioned in the Qur'an, it was left to later generations of scholars to specify exactly how it should be performed. The Qur'an in Sura 5:6 states that people should be purified before they pray and the *Shariah* lays down in minute detail how washing before prayer is to be performed. While the Qur'an mentions prayer twice or thrice a day, the custom of the community, backed by *Hadith*, settled on five prayers daily, in the morning, around noon, in the afternoon, in the evening and at night. When the time for public prayer approaches the muezzin at the mosque will recite the call to prayer or *Adhan,* in Arabic, with the words:

> God is most great. I testify that there is no god but God. I testify that Muhammad is the Prophet of God. Come to prayer. Come to prosperity. God is most Great. There is no god but God.

While prayer can be performed anywhere that is clean, prayer in the mosque is regarded as meritorious.

Attendance at the mosque for congregational prayer at noon on Friday is obligatory for adult male Muslims.

Salat is a combination of several repetitions of fixed postures: standing, bowing, kneeling and prostrating, and the repetition of set prayers and passages from the Qur'an. The worshipper may also insert optional prayers at certain parts of the ritual. *Salat* is obligatory for all Muslims, though certain relaxations are allowed for travellers and the sick. There are many other types of prayer apart from the obligatory *Salat*, prayers in time of need or danger, prayers at burial, prayers for guidance, prayers of repentance and prayers of praise. There are also prayers which are said to win the worshipper special merit and prayers for forgiveness of sins.

Almsgiving

The second religious duty set down in the *Shariah* is that of giving Alms or Charity. This is an obligation that is frequently mentioned in the Qur'an alongside the obligation to pray. The obligatory Almsgiving is called *Zakat* and it came to be fixed at one fortieth of a person's annual wealth. The *Shariah* goes into extensive detail about what is taxable and how the tax should be paid as well as laying down the minimum amount of wealth below which no *Zakat* is payable. It also specifies who should benefit from *Zakat* including the poor and needy, travellers, debtors and slaves working to buy their liberty. There is a further type of charity mentioned in the Qur'an called *Sadaqa*. This term denotes charity given over and above the obligations of *Zakat*. The giving of *Sadaqa* is regarded as something that wins merit in the sight of God.

Fasting

A third religious obligation is *Saum*, which is fasting during the lunar month of Ramadan. The regulations of the *Shariah* specify that the fast should begin with the appearance of the new moon at the start of that month and end with the appearance of the next new moon. During this time, in the hours of daylight, Muslims are forbidden to eat or to drink, to bathe, to smoke, to take snuff or have sexual intercourse. This fast is mandatory for all Muslims over the age of puberty, with certain exceptions including the sick, the feeble-minded, the aged, and pregnant and nursing women. Travellers can be excused for the duration of their journey but, like the sick, they are required to make up for the number of days lost at a later date.

Muslims often explain the purpose of the fast as something that provides training and discipline in self-control. They also suggest that everyone in the community going hungry and thirsty will mean that rich people will be sharing the same experience as the poor and will be more sympathetic and generous towards them because of this. The *Shariah* also makes mention of other voluntary types of fasting which can win merit or the forgiveness of sins.

Pilgrimage

The fourth religious duty regulated by the *Shariah* is the Pilgrimage to Mecca, known as *Hajj*. This is an obligation for all adult Muslims as long as they are of sound mind, in good health and able to make provision for their dependents. As we have seen, the command to perform the Pilgrimage is to be found in the Qur'an. The details of what must be done are set out in the *Shariah* and are reputedly based on the actions of Muhammad on his own final pilgrimage. The object of the Pilgrimage is the

Kaaba, the cubical stone temple in Mecca, reputedly built by Abraham. It was a centre of pilgrimage in pre-Islamic times and some of the rites performed during *Hajj* reflect those of that era.

The following are a few of the obligations set down in the *Shariah*. As pilgrims approach the city of Mecca, they put on special pilgrim clothing, two plain unsewn sheets for every man and white clothing for every woman. From this point on the pilgrims have to observe certain restrictions such as not shaving. At the Kaaba itself pilgrims walk seven times round the building and, near it, walk or run between two small hills, in imitation of Hagar's search for water when she was in the desert with her son Ishmael.

On the seventh day of the Pilgrimage, an Imam preaches a sermon instructing pilgrims in the rituals that they are later to carry out. On the eighth day the pilgrims make for a place called Mina and on the next day to a plain below the hill of Arafat. There they stand in prayer from dawn till sunset. On their return to Mina stones are thrown at pillars which represent the Devil and animals are sacrificed. The final act of the Pilgrimage is walking a further seven times around the Kaaba. However, it is customary, and considered meritorious, also to visit the tomb of the Prophet in Medina. A pilgrimage to Mecca outside the time of the *Hajj* is known as the *Umrah* and is considered a meritorious act.

These four duties, Prayer, Almsgiving, Fasting and Pilgrimage, along with the Confession of Faith, that there is no god except God and that Muhammed is the Prophet of God are so central to Islam that they constitute what Muslims call 'The Five Pillars of Islam'.

Social and Economic Obligations

As well as setting down religious duties, the *Shariah* also lays down a code of regulations to govern and guide Muslims in their social and economic dealings both with fellow Muslims and with non-believers.

It has much to say about marriage. Muslims are encouraged to marry. There is a *Hadith* that states that when Muslims marry, they perfect half of their faith. As we have seen, the Qur'an permits a man to marry up to four women, if he can treat them fairly. The *Shariah* lays down certain prohibitions on marriage on the grounds of consanguinity and affinity. It prescribes no form of religious ceremony for marriage, and none is necessary to make a marriage valid. All that is required is for the man and woman to give mutual consent before two reliable witnesses. The *Shariah* regulates the practice of the giving of a gift to the wife from the husband and specifies under what circumstances it can be returned. It also lays down the mutual duties of husband and wife. It requires the husband to provide for his wife or wives and to treat her, or them, kindly and fairly. It also empowers a husband to punish a wife for disobedience, on the grounds that it is the duty of a wife to obey her husband in all things lawful.

The *Shariah* recognizes the institution of slavery and has regulations for its practice. By its guidance, Muslims are enjoined to show kindness to their slaves and the freeing of slaves is regarded as meritorious.

The *Shariah* has regulations for inheritance. At least two thirds of a person's estate must be passed on to heirs and the portion due to each is specified. Generally, for example, daughters are allocated half what is allocated to sons. There are regulations which govern the killing of animals for meat. The animal must have its throat cut while the words 'In the name of God. God is most great' are pronounced and the blood is drained. Meat not slaughtered in this way, as well as the flesh of some other animals such as pigs are prohibited, or *haram,* to Muslims. Also prohibited are gambling and all forms of intoxicating drinks.

The *Shariah* has regulations about how sales and bargains can be made. It stipulates that both buyer and seller must be of full age, sound mind and free. Hoarding grain to force up the price is forbidden. Usury, lending money for interest, is forbidden. Debts, loans, hire, lease, rental, and wages, as well as pledging, pawning sureties, donations and endowments are also regulated.

There is also a section of the *Shariah* which lays down punishments for certain offences. Probably the most widely known are stoning to death for adultery, whipping for drunkenness and the cutting off of the right hand for theft, though nowadays any practice of these punishments is limited to a few states.

SECTION 2

DEVELOPMENT AND DIVERSITY

Chapter 15

The Rightly Guided Caliphs

Abu Bakr

During the centuries that the Scholars of Islam were developing the *Shariah* the Islamic Community had grown, spread and lost its political unity. From being what it had been under Muhammad, a community with an association of confederated tribes and confined to Arabia, it had expanded to control a vast territory, from Spain in the West to the boundaries of India in the East. It had also undergone major changes in the way it was governed and eventually experienced the political divisions and religious schisms that are partly responsible for the diverse ways in which Islam finds expression today. Starting with Muhammad's immediate successors, the following chapters will attempt to describe and explain some of the circumstances in which this happened, some of the reasons for it and some of its most important consequences.

Muhammad had made no provision for who should succeed him as leader of the *Umma* on his death, but this issue was quickly decided. A group of Muhammad's closest companions, though not including Ali, Muhammad's ward and son-in-law, speedily appointed Abu Bakr, who had been one of Muhammad's first male converts, oldest friend, chief adviser and father-in-law. The title that Abu

Bakr and his successors took was Caliph (successor) of the Prophet of God, or more simply, Caliph. The Caliphs did not take on Muhammad's role as God's Prophet, the revelations were believed to have been completed by the time of his death, but they took over as leader of the Community, commander-in-chief of the army, chief arbiter of disputes, the highest legal authority and controller of the treasury.

Abu Bakr and the three Caliphs who succeeded him were all men who had been close companions of the Prophet and are known to history as the *Rashidun* or 'Rightly Guided' Caliphs. Their rule is widely regarded by Muslims as the Golden Age of Islam, the time when the Islamic Community was at its most ideal. It was under their rule that the Islamic Community first spread beyond Arabia and that arrangements for the government of the new territories were first made.

Before that could happen though the position of the Community in Arabia itself had to be made secure. When Bedouin tribes heard of the death of Muhammad, many broke off ties with the Community, refusing to pay *zakat* on the grounds that their agreement had been with Muhammad alone and not with the Community. In response to this Abu Bakr raised an army of Muslims and the tribes which had tried to break off relations were subdued. The result of this so-called 'War of Apostasy' was to establish Islamic control over the whole of Arabia permanently.

Once all of Arabia was secured, Abu Bakr decided to extend the control of the Islamic Community further. In 634, in order to do this, he called on Muslims to launch attacks on the countries on its borders. One army was dispatched towards Syria and one towards Iraq. Syria was part of the Byzantine Empire, which had its capital in

Constantinople. Although this empire was stable and efficiently governed it had its weaknesses. In its two most important provinces, Syria and Egypt, the Byzantines were extremely unpopular. This was so partly because of the heavy taxes that they levied but partly also because they had a policy of persecuting as heretical the branches of the Christian churches to which most Egyptians and Syrians belonged. Soon the Muslim army was having so much success in Syria and in neighbouring Palestine that the Byzantine Emperor, Heraclitus, was forced to send a huge force against the invaders. However, in a decisive battle near Jerusalem in 634 the Muslims were victorious and were able to take control of Palestine.

Umar

Not long after this Abu Bakr died, to be succeeded by another of Muhammad's oldest companions, Umar ibn al-Khattab. The title most favoured by Umar was 'Commander of the Faithful', and it was as commander of the Muslim forces that he pursued Abu Bakr's policy of expansion. He continued the campaign in Syria and by 635 its capital Damascus had fallen to the Muslims. Once again Emperor Heraclitus raised an army to try to expel the invaders from his former territories but in 636, at a battle fought at Yarmuk, his forces were decisively defeated. The following year the holy city of Jerusalem was handed over to the Muslims and by the year after that the whole of Syria was under Muslim control.

The next issue to face Umar was to make arrangements for the control of the areas that had come under Muslim domination. When the fighting had been going on in Syria, he had made it clear that he was at war only with their Byzantine overlords and not with the common people of Syria themselves. When Umar and his forces took control of the territory, they promised its people that as long as a tribute, or *jizya*, was paid to the Muslim government it would protect the safety of their cities and their lives, their possessions and their places of worship. Jewish and Christian communities, by paying this tribute, were given the status of 'protected minority' or *dhimmi*, and were allowed to keep their own customs, religious practices and laws.

As well as making arrangements for the peoples newly under his control, Umar also had to make provision for the Arab armies which had carried out the conquest. To do this he granted to each Arab soldier a pension based on the time of his conversion to Islam. This made his troops financially independent and able to devote their whole time to military service. In order to cut down friction between the Arab troops and the people of occupied territories he insisted that, in times of peace, they should reside in their own encampments. He did not allow Arabs to own land outside of Arabia and, added to the fact that soldiers were allowed to keep four fifths of anything they captured in war, this ensured that the Caliph always had a force at his disposal ready, willing and able to fight.

Having secured Syria, Umar focused on winning control of the Persian province of Iraq. The once mighty Persian empire was at that time in decline. It had suffered a major defeat at the hands of the Byzantines in 628 and its government was in a state of disunity with several rivals for the throne. The Persian state religion of Zoroastrianism was unpopular with many non-Persians and the peasantry were taxed heavily. It was against this weakened empire that Umar ordered an attack in 638. Soon the capital Ctesiphon had fallen and its king, Yazdegerd, was forced to flee eastward, deeper into Persia, leaving Iraq in Muslim control.

In the following year Umar's generals persuaded him to authorize an attack on Egypt and by 640 most of its rural areas were in Muslim hands. The next year a truce was agreed by terms of which Byzantine troops and officials would evacuate the city of Alexandria within eleven months. This then left the whole of Egypt under Islamic control by September 642.

With the conquest of Egypt so easily accomplished Umar was once again persuaded by his generals to authorize a further attack on the Persian Empire. King Yazdegerd put up strong resistance but the defeat of his armies that year at the battle of Nihawand brought even more of Persia into the Muslims' realm. In 644. Umar was murdered in Medina but by then Syria, Palestine, Egypt, Iraq and most of Persia belonged to the domain of the Caliph. It is a mark of the greatness of Umar that territory so quickly gained was so efficiently governed.

Uthman

Umar's final act as he lay dying was to choose a committee of six men to elect his successor. Once again Ali was overlooked and the office was given to another of Muhammad's close companions, Uthman ibn Affan who belonged to the important Qurayshite Umayyad family from Mecca. Under Uthman's leadership the expansion of the Islamic Empire continued. His governor in Syria built a fleet on the Mediterranean Sea and took the islands of Rhodes and Cyprus while his land forces pushed northwards to Armenia. His governor in Egypt raided as far west as Tunisia, and in Persia Yazdegerd was finally defeated.

However, it was under Uthman that the Community experienced its first serious disputes. The Caliph was accused of using his position to secure positions of power for his relatives. The governor of Syria, Mu'awiyyah, the son of Abu Sufyan, was his cousin. The Governor of Egypt was replaced by Umar's foster brother. It was also rumoured that the Caliph was awarding lucrative supply contracts to members of his own family. In addition to this, he had difficulty in paying his troops their pensions and there were mutinies in Egypt and Iraq. In 656 mutinous troops appeared in Medina and, in a confused situation, a number of them killed Uthman in his house, with the people of Medina, including Ali, unable, or as some of Uthman's supporters said, unwilling to protect him.

Ali

On the death of Uthman, Ali was acclaimed Caliph by the mutineers and the people of Medina alike. He certainly had a strong claim to the office being Muhammad's son-in-law as well as his ward and cousin. There were many people who believed that he should have been the first rather than the fourth Caliph. However, his election was not supported by everyone. The Governor of Syria, Mu'awiyyah, refused to recognize Ali as Caliph and held him responsible for Uthman's death, claiming the right of a kinsman to avenge him. He claimed that Ali had in fact connived at the murder and had done nothing to bring the killers to justice.

For his safety Ali moved his court to the military garrison town of Kufa in Iraq, where support for him was strong. When Mu'awiyyah continued his opposition, Ali deposed him from his governorship in Syria. When Mu'awiyyah refused to accept this decision, Ali felt compelled to move against him. The armies of the two men met at Siffin on the upper River Euphrates in July in 657 and Muslim faced Muslim on the field of battle.

Tradition states that when the battle was going against Mu'awiyyah, he ordered his men to fix leaves of the Qur'an to their spears and call out, 'Let the law of God decide'. It goes on to state that many of Ali's supporters were unwilling to fight on in the circumstances and that he was forced to accept that his dispute with Mu'awiyyah should be put to arbitration on the basis of the teaching of the Qur'an. The judgement that followed went against Ali and recommended that he should abdicate. This Ali refused to do, but his position as Caliph had been weakened.

The arbitration also brought Ali trouble from some of his own most fervent supporters. A group claimed that, in submitting to arbitration, Ali had shown disloyalty to God and as a result they broke away from him. The people of this faction are known to history as the Kharijites or Seceders and they formed the first, but by no means the last, faction to break away from the main Community of Muslims. The Kharijites left Ali and migrated to Nahrawan, in central Iraq, where they made so much trouble for him that he was forced to move against them and in 659 many of them were massacred.

Meanwhile Mu'awiyyah had taken advantage of these troubles of Ali to strengthen his position. His forces took Egypt from Ali's control and he had himself proclaimed Caliph in Jerusalem. For their part the Kharijites turned to terrorist tactics and plotted to assassinate both Ali and Mu'awiyyah. In Kufa in 661 one of their number stabbed Ali to death, thus bringing to an end the line of 'Rightly Guided' Caliphs. Mu'awiyyah survived a stabbing attack and lived to found the next dynasty of Caliphs, known as the Umayyads, who ruled the *Umma* from their capital in Damascus, in modern day Syria.

Chapter 16

Diversity within Islam

Just as is the case with Christianity, Islam has not remained united but has split into different divisions. From early in the Islamic era groups of Muslims have separated themselves from the main body of the faithful for political or doctrinal reasons and formed parties and sects with their own distinctive beliefs and practices. The purpose of this chapter is to explain some of the events and issues that have brought this about and the characteristics of the main group that has emerged.

One issue which has been a point of disagreement is the question of how the Community should be led. In the previous chapter it was stated that Muhammad was succeeded by the four 'Rightly Guided Caliphs'. By far the largest body of Muslims, usually referred to as orthodox or Sunni, accepts that this was the legitimate line of succession. The Sunni position is that the prophethood of Muhammad was God's final act in revealing his message to mankind and that no leader can now have any role in transmitting anything further.

Another issue that has divided opinion among Muslim groups is the question of who should count as belonging to the Community of believers. Generally, the Sunni have taken a tolerant and inclusive position, counting as Muslim everyone who professes faith in the one God and in Muhammad as His Prophet. This attitude has, through history, not been accepted by all people who call themselves Muslims and by their rejection of this, and other beliefs held by Sunnis, they have moved away from the main body of the faithful.

The first example of a group to do this were the Kharijites mentioned in the previous chapter. Having broken away from Ali following the Battle of Siffin, they developed the doctrine that leadership did not need to be in the hands of a Caliph and that ultimately authority belonged to the Community of believers itself. They also developed the idea that all the people of the world could be divided into two groups, those who belonged to their sect, 'The people of Paradise' and everyone else, 'The People of Hell'. Also, contrary to the majority in the *Umma* who held that it is only God, who will judge people on Judgement Day, that can decide who is a true Muslim, the Kharijites taught that anyone who had committed a great sin should be excluded from the Community and its protection.

The extremism and intolerance of the Kharijites brought them into conflict with the main Community and few in Arabia survived the repression that followed. However, the questions their movement raised, such as how should the *Umma* be led and, who can be deemed to belong to it, illustrate issues that have brought about diversity within Islam and among Muslims. The Kharijites were also later to play a part of the story of Islam in North Africa.

The Shia

The most significant group to have broken away from Sunni Islam has been the Shia. Shi-ism had its origins as a political party, but over time built up a series of beliefs which transformed it into a religious movement, with its own distinctive doctrines and practices. There follows a description of the events that brought about this transformation and an examination of the distinctive beliefs of this form of Islam.

The issue that brought the Shia into being was a disagreement over who should lead the *Umma*. As explained in the previous chapter there were a group of Muslims who had believed that Ali, Muhammad's close kinsman, should have been the first Caliph. Ali attracted a group of supporters who took the name of *Shia'tu Ali,* the Party of Ali. On one occasion they took an oath to be friends with those whom Ali befriended and enemies to those to whom he was hostile. Many of his most loyal supporters were in the army garrison town of Kufa in Iraq and it was there that Ali moved his court during his dispute with Mu'awiyyah.

When Ali was assassinated, it was veneration for him, and because they had no desire to be dominated by the Umayyad Mu'awiyyah, that led his supporters to swear an oath of allegiance to Hasan, the son of Ali and Muhammad's daughter Fatima. They promised to support him as Caliph and were deeply disappointed when, after negotiations with Mu'awiyyah, Hasan chose to renounce any claim to the Caliphate. He retired to private life in Medina, where he died a few years later, murdered on the orders of Mu'awiyyah, according to his supporters.

On the death in turn of Mu'awiyyah, in 680 Husayn, the brother of Hasan, was invited by the men of Kufa to join them to lead a rebellion against the new Umayyad Caliph, Yazid. On his way to Kufa with most of his family he was intercepted outside the city by Yazid's forces on the plain of Kerbala. When he refused to swear loyalty to the Caliph, he and most of his family were massacred. This proved a most significant event for the development of the religious ideas and practices of the Shia. The martyrdom of Husayn did much to heighten their veneration of the family of Ali. To this day the anniversary of the slaughter is commemorated on the days culminating on the tenth day, *Ashura,* of the Islamic month of *Muharram.* On that day a passion play re-enacts the tragedy of Kerbala amid extravagant expressions of deep grief and mourning. This sense of sorrow and intense devotion to their three martyrs, Ali, Hasan and Husayn is an essential element in Shi-ism.

It was around this time that a further distinctive feature of Shi-ism was being developed, namely that the rightful leader of the Community, to whom they gave the title Imam, inherited special powers along with the office. The person who can be credited with the spread of this idea was a man called Mukhtar. As agent of Husayn's half-brother, Muhammad al-Hanifiyya, he claimed that the descendants of Ali had a divine right to leadership. Though a revolt against the Umayyads in 684 was a failure it was significant in that, for the first time it attracted to Shi-ism people who were not Arabs. The idea of a divinely elected leader appealed to many Persians, who before the coming of Islam had held the tradition of divine kingship. Over a long period, the Shi-ite movement attracted Persians and others who were dissatisfied with the rule of the Sunni Caliphs, and in this way Shi-ism acquired features that were not Arab in origin.

Another belief that is characteristic of some branches of Shi-ism was exemplified in the year 700 when Muhammad al-Hanifiyya died. Some of his supporters came to believe that he was not actually dead, but had gone into hiding and would appear at a time of great crisis as the *Mahdi* or Rightly Guided One, who would set all wrongs right and re-establish peace and justice on earth.

Diversity within Shi-ism

The Shia history of misfortune continued when the Umayyad dynasty was overthrown in 750. Though the Shia had played a significant part in the downfall of their old rivals, they were given no reward by the Abbasid Caliph who took over leadership of the *Umma* and moved its capital to Baghdad in Iraq.

It was during the time of the Abbasid dynasty, and during the ninth century c.e. in particular, that the Shi-ite ideas mentioned earlier became moulded into doctrinal systems. The fundamental difference between Sunni belief and that which developed among Shia circles concerned the question of the leader of the Community. According to Shia doctrine the Imam is not merely the leader of the Community but also the agent of God's illumination for the world during his age. The Shia belief was that God had chosen the House of Ali to carry the spark of divine light which had passed from prophet to prophet throughout history. They believed that, by carrying this godly light, the Imam was different from the rest of humanity. Bearing this spark of God's wisdom rendered him clean of all sin and endowed him with superior powers.

Shi-ite Muslims believe that it is to the Iman that is given the power to mediate God's revelation to mankind and that without the Iman the meaning and relevance of God's revelation cannot be fully known. A common strand in Shia teaching has been that special knowledge, originating with Muhammad and transmitted to Ali, has been passed on from Imam to Imam. Shi-ism has profoundly offended the Sunni by asserting that the first three Caliphs, whom the Sunni greatly revere, were illegitimate usurpers, and by including a ritual cursing of them into some of their rituals. So important is their belief in the Imam to the Shi-ites that they regard it as an additional 'Pillar of Islam'.

However not all Shi-ites have agreed on the identity of who all have carried this divine light, and this has been a cause of division within Shia Islam itself. The main division, known as the Imamis, recognizes a succession of twelve Imams descended from Ali and Fatima. They believe that this line of Imams came to an end in about 880 with the disappearance of their twelfth Imam, Muhammad al-Mahdi. They wait for his return to restore justice and righteousness on earth. While belief in a coming Mahdi has a place in Sunni Islam, it is much stronger within Shi-ism though once again the various Shia groups do not agree on his identity.

The second largest division of the Shia reveres the same line of succession as do the Imamis as far as the sixth one. This group believes that the legitimate seventh Imam was a man named Ishmael. As they believe that he was the last known Imam, they are known as the Ishmaelis or 'Seveners'. Because this sect seems to have operated as something of a secret society and allowed its members to hide their true commitment in times of danger, very little of its early history is known. It is likely though that during the ninth century the movement was active underground.

During this formative period for them the Ishmaelis came to develop the doctrine that, though the Imam for the age was hidden, he was in touch with the world though the person of an agent, or *wali*. It is among the various Ishmaeli sects that the most extreme beliefs about the importance of the Imams were to be found, such as the doctrine that they are actually incarnations of the Godhead. Among some Ishmaeli groups Muhammad was thought of as just one of a series of emanations of God, thus denying him the unique place that he has in the eyes of Sunni Muslims.

The *Sunna* of the Prophet Muhammad is however still important for Shia Muslims and serves as an authority for religious law, although they do have their own collection of *Hadith* to support their distinct beliefs and observances. When it comes to the practice of religion,

Shia differs only slightly from Sunni Islam. Shi-ites observe the 'Five Pillars of Islam' with differences from the Sunni on only on a few points of detail.

Shia groups have at times enjoyed political success. It was an Ishmaeli, who had declared himself Mahdi, whose successors founded the Fatimid dynasty based in Cairo which for nearly two hundred years challenged the Abbasid Caliphs for control of the Islamic world. In 1502 Imami Shi-ism was declared the official religion of Iran, and remains as such to this day. It is also strong in parts of Iraq. An Ishmaeli group has a presence in Zanzibar and on parts of the East African coast but Ishmaelis today constitute only a small fraction of all Shia who, in turn, account for only about ten percent of Muslims world-wide.

Chapter 17

The Development of Islamic Theology

The Mutazilites

As the Islamic Empire spread, many centres of Greek learning such as those in Syria, Egypt and Iraq were brought under its control and Muslim scholars learned about the ideas and methods of the great Greek scholars of antiquity. At the beginning of the ninth century, an Abbasid Caliph, al-Mamun encouraged an upsurge of interest in Greek scholarship when he ordered that major works on medicine, astronomy, mathematics and philosophy be translated into Arabic. The philosophical works of Aristotle, Plato and others became readily available and widely known. Muslim scholars began not only to study them but also to apply their philosophical ideas and logical methods of thinking to questions of Islamic theology. This group of scholars became known as the Mutazilites. Their attempts to apply these Hellenistic ways of thinking to their own religion raised questions about three issues basic to the faith of Islam; the nature of God, the nature of the Qur'an and the relationship between God and man. Though the answers to these questions that the Mutazilites arrived at were ultimately rejected by them, the challenge that they posed forced the orthodox scholars to work out, and explain in detail, their own answers.

The Mutazilites, sometimes referred to as the Rationalists because of their reliance on reason, were not a sect and counted both Sunni and Shia among their number. The name they gave themselves was, 'The People of Unity and Justice'. They were of the opinion that the idea of the

Unity of God was being undermined by the way that Islamic scholars of the time were speaking and thinking about Him. It was commonly held that God had ninety-nine 'Beautiful Names', including, 'The Knowing', 'The Powerful', 'The Willing', 'The Living' and 'The Speaking'. Some orthodox theologians were suggesting that God had eternal attributes corresponding to these names and used language like, the 'Eternal Knowledge of God' and the 'Eternal Power of God'. To the Mutazilites, talk of these attributes of God being eternal seemed to present a challenge to the idea of the Unity of God, that God was undivided. They were unwilling to talk of God's knowledge being eternal in case it implied the existence of something called God's Eternal Knowledge when the only entity with eternal existence is God Himself. They preferred to say that it was in the essence of God to have knowledge.

The central issue of this controversy between the Mutazilites and the orthodox scholars about the Unity of God came to concern whether the speech of God, the Qur'an, should be thought of as eternal and uncreated, or not. The standpoint of the orthodox was that the speech of God had no beginning, and no ending. They held that the Qur'an had existed, on a tablet in heaven, from eternity and was therefore uncreated.

This belief was an offence to the Mutazilites. The idea that there could be something that was coeval and coexistent with God, they argued, implied not one God but two, or at least that the idea of the Unity of God was being compromised. They insisted that God's speech, the Qur'an, must be regarded as created at a point in time. Moreover, they did not like the idea that God's speech was eternal. If that were so, they reasoned, it would necessarily limit God to having to act in accordance with his speech. Beyond that they thought it ridiculous that the words in the Qur'an addressed to Moses, 'Take off your shoes', could be thought to have existed when Moses himself did not exist. They concluded that it was only logical to assume that commands, like this one, that appear in the Qur'an must have come into existence at the time at which they were spoken, and therefore that the Qur'an must be considered to be created.

Furthermore, to protect the idea of the Unity of God, the Mutazilites rejected any ways of speaking about Him in anthropomorphic terms. For example, they denied that the statement in the Qur'an that believers would see God with their eyes in Heaven should be taken literally. They did this based on the philosophical assumption that because God was infinite, He could not be thought of as having physical characteristics bound by time and space. This belief led them to state that references in the Qur'an to the throne, eyes, hands and face of God needed to be taken figuratively rather than literally. This offended the orthodox theologians who insisted that the words of the Qur'an had to be taken in their literal sense.

The Mutazilites contended that the idea of the Justice of God was endangered by the teaching of the orthodox that it is God who is responsible for all people's acts, and at the same time will reward people in Heaven or punish them in Hell for committing them. The Mutazilites took the view that it was unthinkable that God, who is worshipped as compassionate and merciful, should punish people for acts that He Himself had ordained. To avoid this, they declared that people themselves had to be regarded as the creators of their own acts, and that their destiny depended on their own doing rather than God's fore-ordination. They believed that, through His revelation, God had given people the guidance they needed for them to attain Paradise and that it was their responsibility to follow it, or not. The Mutazilites worked on the philosophical assumption that God must necessarily be just, and were most anxious that He should not be associated in any way with evil. Furthermore, influenced by Greek philosophy, they asserted that good is good and evil is evil of themselves, and not because God had ordained them to be. Indeed, they asserted that God Himself distinguished between good and evil in accordance with reason.

Although the theological ideas of the Mutazilites were seemingly more liberal and open than those of the orthodox theologians, in practice they showed themselves to be harshly dogmatic and intolerant of views other than their own. When in 825 the Abbasid Caliph al-Mamun adopted their position as the official one at his court, the Mutazilites used their influence to have it forcibly imposed on others. In 833 the Caliph required his judges and scholars to give their assent to the Mutazilite doctrine that the Qur'an was created rather than eternal, on pain of dismissal if they refused. This continued till 847 when a new Caliph abandoned the Mutazilite cause.

Chapter 18

The Development of Islamic Theology II

The Reply of the Orthodox

Through using reason rather than revelation as the ultimate standard by which to judge religious truth, the Mutazilites developed doctrines about God, about the Qur'an and about predestination that were very different from those of the orthodox Islamic theologians. Though these doctrines never enjoyed much support among ordinary believers, their very logicality demanded an answer. It was the efforts of the orthodox scholars to counter the challenge of the doctrines of the Mutazilites that led to the development of Islamic theology in its classical form. In order to refute the arguments of the dissenters, the orthodox increasingly adopted the methods of their opponents and in the process Islamic theology was given a logical basis.

The scholar who was most responsible for providing the decisive and definitive answer to the challenge of the Mutazilites was Abu'l Hasan al-Ashari. Born in Basra in Iraq in 873, he studied under a leading Mutazilite teacher there. He was reckoned himself to be one of the most eminent exponents of the Mutazilite doctrines when, in 912, he broke away from his master and became the main defender of orthodoxy.

Even before al-Ashari orthodox scholars had opposed the ideas of the Mutazilites. They accused their opponents of dualism. They argued that the Mutazilites themselves undermined the idea of the Unity of God when they insisted that people had the power to create their own deeds. If this were so, the orthodox argued, they would be encroaching on the power of God who, they held, is the only Creator. They also accused the Mutazilites of trying to limit the power of God when they insisted that He must necessarily do what is best for mankind. They accused them of setting up human reason as the ultimate value, above the Word of God.

One notable defender of the supreme place of the Word of God was ibn Hanbal, the founder of the Hanbalite School of Law. He was one of the *Ulema* who had been dismissed, and tortured, during the Mutazilites' time of power for refusing to give up his belief in the uncreated nature of the Qur'an. He declared that statements in the Qur'an concerning 'the Hand of God' and 'the Face of God', had to be taken literally, and not explained as figurative as the Mutazilites had done. At the same time, he stated that these and other anthropomorphic statements should be accepted without asking questions about the sense in which they should be understood.

The Arguments of al-Ashari

These arguments were taken up by al-Ashari who used the methods of logical reasoning that the Mutazilites had introduced to refute the doctrines that they had developed. He listed his differences with his opponents on four main points. Firstly, following ibn Hanbal, he held that the Qur'an was uncreated. He wrote,

> If anybody says, 'Tell us, do you believe that God's Word is on the Preserved Tablet?' the answer is, 'that is what we believe because God has said, "yet it is a glorious Qur'an written on the Preserved Tablet."'

Secondly, in contrast to the Mutazilites and in agreement again with ibn Hanbal, he insisted that anthropomorphic phrases in the Qur'an must simply be accepted. He criticized the Mutazilites for denying that God has a face despite God saying Himself in the Qur'an that He does. He criticized them too for stating that, if their logic was followed, God would have neither power nor knowledge, nor hearing or sight. His verdict was that Mutazilites created a formula without being able to give sense to it. He wrote,

> One of their leaders has said, 'Allah's Knowledge is Allah and Allah is Knowledge.' So he denies Allah's Knowledge while seeming to acknowledge it, for if Allah's Knowledge is Allah Himself, he ought to say, 'Knowledge forgive me'.

Thirdly he insisted that statements about the last things should be taken as they stand and not explained as figurative. With the regard to the statement in the Qur'an that believers will see God in heaven he wrote,

> If anyone should ask, 'Why not interpret "looking towards their God" as, "looking toward the reward of their God"'? The answer is that it is forbidden to take the Qur'an in anything but its plain sense.

Fourthly, to answer the charge of the Mutazilites that to say that God was the creator of people's deeds would seem to make God guilty of injustice, al-Ashari formulated the concept of 'Acquisition'. The idea behind this concept was that though God was indeed the real and only creator of everything, including people's actions, by actually performing the deeds people acquire responsibility for them. (If this distinction seems unclear to the reader, he or she might take consolation from the fact that there was an Arabic saying, 'More obscure than the Acquisition of the Asharites'.)

Though many of al-Ashari's critics thought that the doctrine of 'Acquisition', whereby people have to accept as their own those things that God has decided they would do, equated to a doctrine of compulsion, al-Ashari considered that this gave people sufficient responsibility for their actions to be justly rewarded or punished the at the Last Judgement. Al-Ashari's concern was above all to maintain that God alone was all powerful, and that nothing could thwart His will. To hold to this fundamental principle, he was prepared to state that God is the creator of all that is evil as well as all that is good although he maintained at the same time that this in no way implied that God was in any way evil.

Ultimately the views of ibn Hanbal, al-Ashari and other like-minded orthodox scholars prevailed within the *Ulema*. Revelation, in the form of the words of the Qur'an, rather than Reason became the ultimate standard by which to judge religious truth. Al-Ashari's teaching and methods became the basis of orthodox Islamic theology which has been essentially conservative rather than speculative throughout the centuries that followed.

Chapter 19

The Sufis I

Origins

In earlier chapters of this book, we have seen how Islamic scholars developed a detailed code of regulations and guidance as to how Muslims should behave. However, from the second century of the Islamic era onwards, some Muslims came to feel that merely performing the requirements laid down in the regulations was not sufficient. They feared that if religion was only a matter of keeping to a code of conduct, it could become empty and formal. Some of them began to look for a deeper meaning behind the law and began to make a distinction between the outward form of the law and its inward significance.

Previous chapters of this book have also described some of the ways in which Islamic theological ideas were developing. It is perhaps not surprising that the formulation of these ideas and the system of doctrine that emerged tended only to attract the interest and attention of a small body of scholarly people. It is understandable that the search of the *Ulema* to find the right way to define the nature of God, and their discussions as to whether the Qur'an was created or uncreated, did not satisfy people who might be looking for the vivid personal relationship, reflected in passages the Qur'an, between God and themselves.

The movement within Islam that has sought to satisfy a believer's desire to have a knowledge of God based on personal experience, rather than merely to know about Him, and to go beyond the regulations of the *Shariah* to the reality that they symbolize, is known as Sufism. The idea of the closeness of God and the possibility of direct experience of Him finds some support in certain passages in the Qur'an. Texts that have been especially significant to Sufi Muslims are, *We are nearer to him than his jugular vein,* Sura 50:16 and, *Wherever you turn, there is the presence of Allah,* Sura 2:115. It is possible to detect how Sufi ideas and practices as they developed have been influenced at times by Persian, Christian, Greek and other external ideas, but essentially Sufism belongs within Islam.

The name given to these mystics, Sufi, may have come from a nickname given to Muslim ascetics who used to wear rough woollen garments, (*suf* is Arabic for wool),

It was among these ascetics that Sufism had its origins. The rulers of the Umayyad dynasty, with their court in Damascus, became notorious for their luxury and loose living, in spite of the example that Muhammad had given. Early conquests had brought immense power and wealth to the rulers of the Islamic Community and they often used it for their ease and pleasure in ways that scandalized many faithful Muslims. This, along with corruption in the court, led an increasing number of pious Muslims to withdraw from society and to renounce all its comforts and pleasures.

Representative of this group of people, and the best known of all the early ascetics, was a man called Hasan al-Basri (d. 728). Typical of their message was these words he wrote to one of the Caliphs, *The more the world pleases you, the more you should be wary of it*. The motivating force behind these ascetics was the idea of the fear of God's judgement, on society and on themselves. With a heavy sense of guilt, they abandoned the pleasures and comforts of this world, which they believed was essentially evil, in the hope of happiness in the next one.

From the second century of the Islamic era there is evidence that the ascetics began to organize themselves collectively. Groups met to recite aloud the Qur'an and a feature of their worship was what they called the commemoration of God, *dhikr*. In this they would repeat in unison the name of God, or some short religious phrase, until a state of ecstasy was attained in which they experienced the nearness of God's presence. In this way they hoped to escape from the evil of the world to a closer communion with the Almighty.

Developments

The second century of the Islamic era also saw a significant development in the ideas of the ascetic movement, when some of their number began to focus not on the fear of God, but on the love of God. One of the early written expressions of this came from an ascetic and mystic poet named Rabia of Basra (d. 728). The dominant note in her poems is not her fear of God but her love of Him. In a famous passage she wrote,

> O God, if I worship Thee in fear of Hell, burn me in Hell, and if I worship Thee in hope of Paradise, exclude me from Paradise, but if I worship Thee for Thine own sake, withhold not Thy Beauty.

She refused offers of marriage because she said that she had in effect ceased to exist. She said, *I have passed out of self. I exist in God altogether*.

These two ideas of the Love of God and losing themselves in the Love of God, came increasingly to motivate the thinking of the Sufi mystics. For them, God was essentially a personal being who could be known by the believer. A

Hadith that they often quoted expresses both the nearness and accessibility of God.

> Neither My Heaven nor My Earth contains Me, but I am contained in the heart of My servant who is a believer.

In seeking to express the reality of the union with God that they felt they could attain, some Sufis used powerful language and imagery that scandalized the orthodox. One Persian mystic taught that to say *I and God* was to deny the reality of God. *Lover, Beloved and Love are One*, he wrote. In his ecstasy he is said to have cried, *Glory to me! How great is my Majesty!* A more sober and scholarly mystic, al-Junaid (d. 911) wrote that it was necessary for man to die to himself and to live in God, and that man would be perfected when he lost himself in the Love of God. A contemporary of his, Mansur ibn Husayn al-Hallaj, went further and stated that man may be thought of as God incarnate and stated *I am the Truth*. In 922 he was executed for blasphemy.

Chapter 20

The Sufis II

A Challenge to Orthodoxy

By the tenth century c.e. relations between the mystics and the orthodox theologians were not good. The explanation for this has much to do with the way in which the leadership of the Sufi movement had changed. The early ascetics were often themselves members of the *Ulema* but, by three centuries after the time of Muhammad, leading figures in the mystic movement increasingly came from people who were less educated and whose qualifications were their personal charisma rather than their learning. The popularity of the mystic movement was growing because of the satisfaction it was giving to people's religious longings, and the fact that it was more likely to accommodate local cultural beliefs and practices. The meetings that they held and the *dhikr* ceremonies that were performed at them were competing with the mosques as centres for worship and community gatherings. The orthodox leaders feared that they might take over from them in importance.

The religious leadership that the *Ulema* claimed over the Islamic community was based on their possession of the knowledge and doctrine which they had acquired through long and arduous study. They were understandably jealously protective of their positions of leadership and believed that what they taught about correct belief and practice was the only proper way. They were afraid that if they relaxed their control this would open the door to heresy and innovation.

These fears that Sufism would lead to heresy were in some cases justified. The mystical experiences of al-Hallaj and others had led them into making statements that, in the eyes of the orthodox were both heretical and blasphemous. The execution of al-Hallaj was an attempt to keep his dangerous ideas in check, but it only led Sufis to be more careful of what they said in public and to clothe their teaching in more hidden and indirect language.

In addition, among certain Sufi groups there was a tendency to take the demands of the *Shariah* lightly. Sufis tended to be more concerned with understanding the meaning behind the regulations rather than the practice of their outer form. By the ninth century there were Sufis who believed that the awareness of the inner reality of the *Shariah* freed them from following its obligations. Some of them came to regard the *Shariah* as a means to an end, something that could lead the believer to a full experience of God, but which could be abandoned when that end had been reached.

Such people rejected the claim of the orthodox *Ulema* that theirs was the only way to God. Through their teaching, their saints and their *dhikr,* the Sufis claimed to offer a direct and personal knowledge and experience of God, not just what they thought was second-hand knowledge provided by the teaching of the theologians. Some even claimed that theology was in fact a barrier to knowing God. By the tenth century the conflict between the two interpretations of Islam seemed irreconcilable.

Al-Ghazali

The man who managed to bridge the gap was Abu Hamid al-Ghazali. Born in 1058, al-Ghazali was schooled as an orthodox theologian and by 1091 he had established himself as one of the greatest scholars of this time, as a professor of theology at the main centre of learning in Baghdad. However, in spite of his learning he found that he could get no personal religious satisfaction from either law or theology and became convinced that God could be found in neither of them. In 1096 he abandoned his scholastic career and spent years searching for something that would give him the spiritual satisfaction that he desired. He eventually turned to the way of the Sufis and first set himself to find out all there was to know about their doctrines. He then decided that the essence of what Sufis taught could only be gained by first-hand experience. So, abandoning wealth and family, he took up the life of a mystic, only interrupted by his writing a series of books in which he tried to reconcile the teachings and practice of Sufism with those of Islamic orthodoxy. The best known of these books is his 'Revival of the Religious Sciences'.

Al-Ghazali is a major figure in the development of Islam. On the one hand, his thorough knowledge of law and theology had the respect of jurisprudists and theologians alike. On the other he understood the way of the Sufis from within this own personal experience. With these two things he managed to find common ground between the two and by so doing he gained a place for Sufi mysticism within Islam beside the legalism of the jurisprudists and the intellectualism of the theologians. The key to this common ground, al-Ghazali taught, was to observe a proper balance between observing the form of the law, the *Shariah,* and recognizing its internal meaning, its *Haqiqa.* He taught that *Haqiqa* without *Shariah* was baseless and that *Shariah* without *Haqiqa* was meaningless. He wrote, *Shariah is to worship God. Haqiqa is to behold Him.* From this time onward Sufism, at least in its sober and law-abiding form, has been accepted within Islam as a reasonable and praiseworthy way of life.

The Brotherhoods

From the twelfth century c.e. Sufi groups began to organize themselves more formally into Brotherhoods, or *turuq* (singular, *tariqa*). At the centre would be a spiritual master who was believed to have a special blessing or *baraka*. He would lead and instruct followers in his path or *tariqa* and its rituals, such as his version of *dhikr,* to a fuller experience of God. These leaders were given the Arabic title of Shaykh or the Persian one of *Pir,* both of which mean 'old man'. When followers reached a certain level of spiritual maturity, they in turn would be given the right to pass on the instruction to their own pupils. Often these people themselves would establish their own branches of the *tariqa*. In this way the Brotherhoods eventually spread throughout the Muslim world. On their deaths some of the most revered Shaykhs were venerated as saints, their birthdays were celebrated, and their tombs became shrines and objects of visits, *ziyara,* by members of their Brotherhood.

The earliest Brotherhood was established in Baghdad by Abd al-Qadiri al-Jilani (1078-1166) and from him it took the name of the Qadiri Order or *Qadiriyya*. Among many other orders was the Shadhili or *Shadhiliyya*. This was based on the leadership of Nur al-Din al-Shadhili (1196-1258). Each of the Brotherhoods developed its own distinctive rituals. The *dhikr* of the *Qadiriyya,* for instance, is marked by its rhythmic repetitive invocation of God, accompanied by strong, rhythmical and regulated breathing. Others favour performing *dhikr* in a more restrained manner.

Because the Brotherhoods tended to be less strict about imposing orthodox beliefs and practices, they were often, though not invariably, more accommodative to local customs, beliefs and practices. Consequently, their brand of Islam with its lively and colourful rituals often proved attractive to new converts.

Just as the *Ulema* were doing with their mosques and their legal guidance, the Brotherhoods with their meetings and their rituals helped, through the centuries, to bind Islamic communities together and to preserve them. This was especially the case in times when governments were weak or divided, or when areas were overrun by invading powers.

SECTION 3

ISLAM COMES TO AFRICA AND TO MALAWI

Chapter 21

Islam comes to North Africa

Initial Conquest

Within 100 years of the establishment of the Islamic Community in Medina, Muslim generals had brought the whole of North Africa under the control of the Caliphs. By 642, only 10 years after the death of Muhammad, the generals of Caliph Umar had defeated the forces of the Byzantine Empire in Egypt and had brought the whole of the country under Islamic military control, though still initially making use of the Byzantine civil service. The majority of Egyptians were Coptic Christians, and as 'People of the Book', they were allowed to keep their religion and culture in return for paying the *jizya* tax. The civil service was gradually Arabized and in 705 Arabic was declared the official language. The Islamization of the majority of the population and their adoption of Arabic as the *lingua franca,* was however a much slower process. This took several centuries and came about largely through the political, educational and economic advantages that being a Muslim conferred, and also from immigration of Arab nomadic tribes-people.

Once Egypt had been secured, Muslim armies launched a series of invasions westward along the coast of North Africa. By the first years of the eighth century, they had extended Muslim control as far as the coast of the

Atlantic, overcoming the forces of the Byzantine Empire which had controlled the coastal zone and subduing resistance from Berber peoples who inhabited the interior. On the coastal strip the Arabization of the civil service and the promotion of the Arabic language proceeded at a quicker pace than in Egypt. Many of the Berbers there joined the Muslim army and it was a Berber general, Tariq ibn Ziyad, with a largely Berber force, who in 711 crossed from Morocco to begin the conquest of Spain on behalf of the Umayyad Caliphs.

Independence from Control of the Caliphs

However, there was widespread discontent among the Berber converts that they were being discriminated against politically, economically and socially by the Arab Muslims. In the 740s this resentment was sparked into a revolt for independence from Arab control by Kharijite missionaries, whose emphasis on the unity of all believers found support from many Berbers. A certain amount of Arab control was reimposed only when the Caliph in Damascus sent a large army from Syria.

However, the independence of all of North Africa's Muslims from the control of the Caliphs was not long delayed. In 750 the Umayyad Dynasty was overthrown by the Abbasids who moved the capital from Damascus in Syria 500 miles eastward to Baghdad in Iraq. North Africa in this way became more remote from the centre of their government and this contributed to the Abbasid Caliphs eventually losing their authority there.

In *Ifriqiya*, modern day Libya, Algeria and Tunisia, Berber discontent at foreign domination continued after the suppression of the Kharijite led rebellion. A governor named ibn al-Aghlab who, in 800, eventually brought peace to the region, was rewarded by the Abbasid Caliph of the day by being given the right for him and his descendants to rule the region in perpetuity. From that time onward Baghdad exercised no authority west of Egypt. The result was the flourishing of an independent North African Islamic state which was an important centre of culture and learning, with a distinctive style of architecture and a navy which controlled much of the Mediterranean Sea.

In 832 the Abbasid Caliph gave away direct control of Egypt. This was taken on by a series of governors who ruled independently of Baghdad. Two of the strongest of them were able to set up their own short-lived dynasties under whom the country, no longer economically exploited by an external power, was able to become militarily strong and prosperous. This lasted till 968 when the country was taken over by Muslims from a different religious tradition, a sect of the Shi-ite Ishmaelis.

The Fatimid Dynasty

In *Ifriqiya* many of the Berber tribes resented the rule of the foreign Aghlabid dynasty and in their struggle for independence from them, yet again, a religious sect played an important part. The Ishmaeli branch of the Shia sect had the ambition of bringing the whole Islamic Community under their Imam. Looking for a base from which to launch this campaign they sent a propagandist from their base in Syria to *Ifriqiya*. There they gained Berber support for their attempts to overthrow the Aghlabids with the promise of a coming *Mahdi*, their leader ibn Husain. On his arrival, and the eventual overthrow of the Aghlabids in 909, ibn Husain was proclaimed Imam and *Mahdi*. As he was descended from Ali and Fatima, the daughter of Muhammad, the dynasty he founded were known as the Fatimids.

In pursuit of their policy of replacing the Abbasids and bringing all Muslims to acknowledge leadership of their Imams as God's rightful representatives, the Fatimids spread their authority as far as Morocco in the west and by 969 had captured Egypt to the east. Four years later they moved into a newly built capital city, Cairo, and from there, for the next two centuries challenged the Sunnite Abbasid Caliphs for supremacy of the Islamic world. At the height of their power, from the Atlantic Ocean to the parts of Arabia that contained the holy cities of Mecca and Medina, the name of the Fatimid Caliph was mentioned in the Friday prayers as the rightful successor of the Prophet. In Cairo in 972 the *al-Azhar* mosque was founded, which later developed into the world's first university. It came under Sunni control after the fall of the Fatimid dynasty in 1171 and has developed into what is acknowledged to this day as the world's most important centres for the study of the Qur'an and Islamic Law.

Long before this the Fatimid's control of *Ifriqiya* was lost when, under pressure from their predominantly Sunnite subjects, the viceroys they had installed there refuted their loyalty to the Fatimid Caliph and declared their spiritual allegiance to the rival Abbasid Caliphate. To punish them, the Fatimid Caliph encouraged two uncivilized nomadic Arab tribes to migrate to *Ifriqiya*, which they did in waves, starting around 1050. Their presence in the region was extremely disruptive as they plundered the wealth of the coastal cities and turned the cultivated land into rough pasture for their sheep and camels. However, through their intermarriage with the Berber tribes-people of the interior it did lead the majority of Berbers to convert to Islam and to adopt the Arabic language.

Chapter 22

Reform Movements in North Africa

The Almoravids

A few Berber tribes in the far west and in the Sahara had remained untouched by the Arab invasion and it was from among these that two notable Islamic reform movements had their origins. Both of these had great consequences for the development of Islam in North Africa itself, in Spain to the north and south across the Sahara to West Africa.

The nomadic Berber Tuareg were a tribe who inhabited the western Sahara Desert and by the tenth century many of them had converted to Islam. The great Muslim traveller and historian ibn Khaldun tells how, around 1035, one of their leaders made a pilgrimage to Mecca. While there he was so shocked at what he thought was the ignorance of his people about true Islam that he brought in a religious teacher to instruct them. This teacher, Abd Allah ibn Yasin, gave a group of followers doctrinal and military training in Morocco in a stronghold (in Arabic, *Ribat*). It was perhaps from this that the people of the movement got their name, *al-Murabitun,* in English, the Almoravids. From their fortress they undertook a militant program of reform, attempting to bring people's lives more in line with the *Shariah*, based strictly on the Malikite School of Law. Once he had united the Tuareg he campaigned at their head to impose his authority over, and to spread the reformation among the rest of the people of Morocco.

In this they were successful and after the death of ibn Yasin his successors, from their newly built capital at

Marrakesh, established a powerful and prosperous Berber empire that included present day Algeria and southern Spain. Its influence even crossed the Sahara to the Kingdom of Ghana as will be explained in the following chapter.

The Almohads

By the twelfth century, the Almoravids had lost much of their reforming zeal and were overcome and succeeded by a second group of puritanical reformists, the Almohads, in Arabic *al-Muwahhidun* (the people who hold to the unity of God). Once again, the movement was founded by a religious scholar. Muhammad ibn Tumert was a Berber theologian who from 1117 started to criticize the beliefs and conduct of the Almoravid leaders. He attacked the Malikite version of the *Shariah* that they followed, insisting that Islamic law should be based only on the Qur'an and the *Hadith*. He also preached against lax moral standards in society, condemning amongst other things, music, dancing and drinking. When he was not initially successful, like ibn Yasin before him, he withdrew to the mountains and gathered support before starting on a campaign to overthrow the Almoravids and reform the moral life of the region.

Between 1130 and 1172, under ibn Tumert and his successors, the Almohads were able to take over all the territory once controlled by Almoravids and advance their control even further into what is now Libya. The time of the Almohads is rightly regarded as the Golden Age of North African civilization. Marrakesh became a beautiful and cultured city. The hospital there was widely acclaimed as the best in the world. Two of the greatest Muslim scholars, ibn Rushd (Averroes) (d. 1038) and ibn

Sina (Avicenna) (d. 1198), wrote under the patronage of the Almohads.

However eventually the Almohads, like the Almoravids before them, lost their vitality and were unable to maintain their authority. Rulers became exploitative and effete, people became discontented, tribal rivalries grew, and governors revolted. By 1275 the Almohad empire had fallen and been, in North Africa, divided into three regions that correspond to modern day Morocco, Algeria and Tunisia.

Chapter 23

Muslims in West Africa, the First Thousand Years

The thousand miles of desert that separate North Africa from the northern parts of West Africa has never been an impenetrable barrier to contact between the two regions. Trade based largely on gold, ivory and slaves going north and salt, copper and blades going south had been carried out at least since Roman times, mostly through the agency of desert Berber tribes. In northern West Africa, even before Muslims came in any numbers, there were flourishing towns and cities and organized networks of trade under kings with developed systems of government.

Following the coming of Islam to North Africa, contacts across the desert increased and by the eighth century c.e. Muslim Berber traders were regularly attending markets in cities at the southern termini of the trade routes, often living there in their own distinct districts. They did not come with the intention of proselytizing, but through them the influence of Islam spread and, particularly among the local trading classes, people began converting to the religion.

The Empire of Ghana

In the vast area between the Sahara Desert and the tropical forests of West Africa, known as the Western Sudan, the first of three major empires to emerge was that of Ghana (not to be confused with the modern country of the same name). From their capital Koumbi Saleh its emperors controlled many vassal states in an area from the River Senegal to the River Niger. Writing in 1067 the Muslim historian al-Bakri described the prosperity of Koumbi Saleh, which had a separate quarter for foreign merchants with twelve mosques and a number of learned Muslim scholars, some of whom were officials at the emperor's court. These men made an important contribution to the spread of literacy and the establishment of Islamic scholarship in the region.

From the tenth century Ghana had been rivalling Berber tribes for control of the southern parts of the most westerly of the trans-Saharan trade routes and when they came to power in Morocco the Almoravids sent forces to campaign across the desert. In 1076 they captured Koumbi Saleh and for ten years were active in Ghana, raiding towns and also trying to impose their religion on the local people. Though they soon withdrew, their presence had two significant results. The first was that some of the vassal rulers converted to Islam, at least nominally. The second was that it helped cause the slow decline and fragmentation of the empire and its eventual take over by the empire of Mali around 1235.

The Empire of Mali

This empire, which eventually stretched from the Atlantic to beyond the River Niger, was founded by Sundiata Kieta who was probably at least a nominal Muslim. Its greatest ruler however, from 1307-1332, was Mansa Musa, a pious Muslim. Such was his wealth, and so extravagant his generosity, it is reported, that while travelling to Mecca to perform the *hajj*, the price of gold fell considerably in Cairo as he passed through. The visit to Mecca had consequences for the development of Islam in his empire. The experience of the Pilgrimage seems to have inspired Mansa Musa's zeal for his religion. He brought back with him experts in Islamic law and began the practice of sending students from Mali to North Africa for advanced studies. One reason for Mansa Musa and other Malian emperors promoting Islam was that the ties that bound fellow Muslims together were useful in promoting trade relationships with Muslims from North of the Sahara and also an amount of unity among a very large, far flung and diverse group of subjects.

Mansa Musa's pilgrimage also brought West Africa to the attention of the wider Muslim world, and beyond. It was visited in the fourteenth century by two great Muslim travellers, ibn Battuta and ibn Khaldun who between them provide an account of the influence of Islam in the empire of Mali at that time. For some people there it involved performing the religious duties and learning the Qur'an by heart. It seemed to these travellers though that for many who called themselves Muslims their traditional way of life, their diet, and their marriage customs had been left more or less untouched by Islam. The majority of people in the empire who lived away from the cities and trading centres, they reported to be completely pagan.

The Empire of Songhai

In the middle of the fifteenth century Mali was eventually overrun by one of its governors, Sonni Ali, who from his capital Gao established the empire of Songhai. Though nominally a Muslim, Sonni Ali thought it important to maintain the loyalty of his subjects, most of whom were traditionalists, by identifying closely with traditional religious beliefs and practices. He was also deeply suspicious of the *Ulema*, fearing that their loyalty to Islam might be stronger than their loyalty to himself. This policy though was reversed by one of his successors, Askia Muhammad a pious Muslim who gave active support to Muslim scholars, seeking their advice and appointing them to government posts.

Under Askia Mohammad Islam prospered as never before in West Africa. When the traveller Leo Africanus visited the city of Timbuktu in 1556, he reported, 'a great store of doctors, judges, priests and other learned men maintained by the king'. In addition to its world-renowned library, Timbuktu is reported to have had 150 mosques. Cities like Timbuktu and Jenne which had long been important centres of learning were further developed and attracted eminent scholars from North of the Sahara. Nevertheless, the Askias of Songhai did not make any sustained attempt to convert their traditionalist subjects to Islam and even practised some of the traditional rites of divine kingship. One of the kings explained to the *Ulema* that not to do so would mean losing the support of many of his subjects.

The empire of Songhai lasted till almost the end of the sixteenth century when its rivalry with Morocco over the control of trans-Saharan trade led to an invasion and defeat by a Moroccan army. The break-up of the empire led to the area being fragmented into a number of smaller states and an end to the generally peaceful conditions in which trade could thrive. This led in turn to a decline in the standard of life, especially in the cities.

Throughout this period though, Islam did survive. The rulers of the states were generally at least nominally Muslims, but the main champions of the religion were the *Ulema*. These men were educated to the highest level and were in close touch with parts of the rest of the Islamic world. They kept alive the traditions of learning and knowledge of the Islamic law, though for a long time they did not feel strong enough to impose it on others, or to challenge rulers who did not try to apply the *Shariah* and who 'mixed' Islamic with traditional practices.

Chapter 24

Muslims in West Africa, the Great Reformers

The situation changed dramatically in northern West Africa from the middle of the eighteenth century when Islamic clerics increasingly laid stress on the uniqueness of Islam and its incompatibility with traditional ways of worship and practice, and who felt that Islam in their area was losing its identity by being mixed with non-Islamic elements. It was from the *Ulema,* that came the people who were largely responsible for a major Islamic revival throughout the region. At the root of this revolution, tribal and economic factors played a part, beside religious ones.

The tribe who had the foremost part to play in this revival were the Fulani. These were pastoralist nomads who had their origins in the region of Senegal but had spread slowly eastward as far as Hausaland in which area the main states, from the sixteenth century, were Kanem and Bornu. These were ruled by Muslims and had their own learned class, but with a fair amount of 'mixing'. Owning cattle, the Fulani were rich and powerful and resented it when rulers imposed taxes on them for passing through or staying in their territory.

An important religious factor in the revival that was to take place was the emergence in West Africa of the Qadiriyya and Tijaniyya Sufi brotherhoods. From across the desert their introduction to the region was largely the work of a clerical family known as the Kunta. The leading member of this family was Sidi al-Mukhtar al-Kabir. He was largely responsible for the promotion of the Qadiriyya and his spiritual authority was acknowledged by its growing number of members throughout the Western

Sudan. The significance of the brotherhoods and their leaders was that the people who had adopted Islam in West Africa up to that time had mostly come from the trading classes, some rulers and, of course, the *Ulema*. All of these had been unwilling, or unable, to prevent people continuing with their traditional beliefs or 'mixing' their practice of Islam with them. With the spread of the brotherhoods there arose a group of Muslims who had a desire to promote what they saw as pure Islam, uncontaminated by being mixed with practices that they thought were incompatible with the true religion. In addition, in order to bring this about, they were prepared to declare *jihad* on rulers who, in their opinion, misled their subjects by allowing this 'mixing'.

This first happened in the region of Futa Jalon in the Senegal region, in the eighteenth century. There two different leaders from one of the Fulani clerical families declared *jihad* against local rulers and set up imamates run on Islamic lines, with the establishment of *madrassas*, Islamic schools, and the *Shariah* administered by *qadis*, Islamic judges. Though neither imamate lasted more than a few decades, a pattern was set which was followed with much greater success in the next century.

Uthman dan Fodio

The first reformer to have major success was a Fulani cleric Uthman dan Fodio from the Hausa state of Gobir. Dan Fodio was highly educated in Islamic theology and law and an initiate of the Qadiriyya Brotherhood. From the age of twenty he began trying to reform society by preaching against the King of Gobir who, though himself a Muslim, was not governing according to the *Shariah*. He criticised the king and his court for corruption, repression, levying non-Islamic taxes, and following traditional royal practices. When the king of tried to supress him, dan Fodio, who was inspired by visions that God was calling him to do so, declared *jihad* against him in 1804. His attack on non-Islamic taxes had appealed to the Fulani pastoralists and his condemnation of corruption and exploitation had won over many of the Hausa peasants. With their support he defeated the king in battle and, taking on the title of 'Commander of the Faithful', began to carry out the reforms he had preached about.

Beyond his own area, he took advantage of the wide network of the Qadiriyya Brotherhood, like minded members of the *Ulema* and also the Fulani, many of whom had not previously been Muslims, but who had felt exploited by the Hausa kings. He sent out his flags to encourage revolt throughout the Hausa region and one by one Hausa states were taken over by his supporters. Though dan Fodio himself was more of a scholar than a ruler, his son Muhammad Bello and his brother Abdullah went on to form states that they set out to run on strictly Islamic lines. To do this they appointed Emirs as governors, *qadis* as judges and *wazirs* as advisers, copying early Islamic practice.

Al-Hajj Umar

To the west of the Hausa states a second great reformer followed the example of Uthman dan Fodio. This was Umar ibn Said Tal. He was also from a Muslim clerical family, and with the highest level of Islamic education. He made the pilgrimage to Mecca in 1824, where he gained the title *al-Hajj*. While in Mecca he met Muhammad al-Ghali the representative of the Tijaniyya Brotherhood, which had originated in North Africa and had already spread across the Sahara. Al-Ghali initiated Umar into the highest level of the Brotherhood and gave him the title of

'Caliph of the Tijaniyya in the Sudan'. During the next decades Umar travelled through Hausaland learning how the states there were administered on Islamic lines, then on westward, all the while trying to persuade Muslims to leave the Qadiriyya and join the Tijaniyya. In his home area in Senegal, he withdrew with his followers to a stronghold to train them up. He stressed to them that before they could take part in holy war, the lesser *jihad*, they had to win the greater *jihad* which was control over their own wills and desires.

In 1852 he declared that God had commanded him to wage *jihad* against all unbelievers and those who mixed their Islamic faith with non-Islamic beliefs and practices. Unable to spread his influence in the area of Senegal because of the expansion at that time of the French colonial power, he turned eastward and within 10 years he had built an empire almost as big as that of Uthman dan Fodio. However, this empire was not as well founded and after Umar's death in 1864 it fragmented as its provincial governors fought amongst themselves. Nonetheless an important result of Umar's career was to establish the Tijaniyya Brotherhood as the most important in the region and, more significantly, along with the efforts of Uthman dan Fodio, to ensure that, to this day, Islam is the dominant religion in the northern part of West Africa.

Chapter 25

Muslims in East Africa, the First Thousand Years

Islam reached East Africa by sea, and the history of the religion in this region belongs much more to its history around the shores of the Indian Ocean than in the rest of Africa. From December to February every year ships have been able to take advantage of the Monsoon winds which blow from the North East down the coast of East Africa, and which, from April to September with equal regularity, blow in the opposite direction. These winds helped to establish round the shores of the Indian Ocean a huge trading circuit that eventually stretched from Mozambique as far east as China.

There are reports of contact between the East African coast and the area of the Arabian Gulf as early as the sixth century b.c.e. Four centuries before the time of Muhammad there are records of Arab merchants sending their trading agents who settled in the Somali region and intermarried with the local women there.

In the early centuries after the establishment of the Islamic Community there are traditions, from both East Africa and Arabia, that attribute increased settlement in East Africa by Arab and Persian Muslims to some of them escaping from persecution that resulted from rivalry for power, failed rebellions and sectarian differences during the Umayyad and Abbasid eras. The most important of these traditions is that of Ali ibn al-Hassan and his six sons. The Kilwa Chronicle is one of six Swahili histories, written down around 1520 but based on older oral traditions. It tells how, in the middle of the tenth century, ibn Hassan, the son by a slave woman of the Sultan of the Persian area of Shiraz, being unable to compete with his brothers in his own country, took his six sons and their families and set off for the East African coast in seven ships. Each is said to have stopped at a different place, including Mombasa and Pemba, and founded a settlement. Ibn Hassan himself is reputed to have stopped at Kilwa on the Tanzanian coast and there to have established a dynasty which lasted until overthrown by the Portuguese at the end of the fifteenth century.

It is widely agreed by historians that it is from about 900 that Islam began to take strong root among the peoples of the East African coast. Part of the reason for this was the spread of Islam at that time around the shores of the Western Indian Ocean. This stimulated a growth of trade and the movement of people throughout this vast area. In this process more people, especially from Arabia and Persia, came to settle on the East African coast and its islands in places like Malindi, Mombasa, Zanzibar and Pemba. There they prospered, wearing cotton from India, drinking out of cups from China and building cities with their mosques, in stone and coral, modelled on those of their original home areas.

Another factor which contributed to the establishment of Islam on the east coast of Africa was the emergence of a new people with their own distinctive society, language and culture. The custom of Arab and Persian men marrying Bantu women had been going on for centuries and their offspring resulted in this new ethnic group, the Swahili. Kiswahili, which became their common language, is based on Bantu grammar but its vocabulary includes many Arabic and Persian words. New immigrants had to learn it in order to become integrated into Swahili society, the religion of which was Islam.

The Shirazi Era

Between the twelfth and fifteenth centuries, known as the Shirazi era, Swahili civilization reached its height. During this period, it was people with links to the Shiraz who were the most dominant influence, winning control of most of the towns from Mogadishu in the Somali region as far south as Sofala on the coast of Mozambique. This increased prosperity of the region was linked to a fresh wave of expansion of Islamic influence along the whole of the Indian Ocean during that period, with the Islamization of coastal cities as far away as Malaysia and Indonesia.

The stimulus to trade that resulted throughout the Indian Ocean caused a further flourishing of Swahili towns and cities which by the fifteenth century are reported to have numbered thirty-seven. One of the most important of these was Kilwa, close to the gold and copper fields of the interior from which it gained great wealth. When ibn Battuta visited, in 1329, he reported a large, fine and well-constructed town, inhabited by pious, black Shafi-ite Muslims, with a large mosque and magnificent palace, inhabited by a sultan who minted his own coins.

There is little evidence from this time that the Swahili made much attempt to move into the interior to trade or to conquer, inhibited by the inhospitable nature of the territory beyond the coast and the hostility of tribes there. Rather they cooperated with some of the tribes of the interior who brought their goods to them, including gold, ivory, animal skins and slaves. The towns generally were politically independent, often feuding to get advantage over each other. Their inability to work together to oppose a foreign intruder was to prove eventually fatal for the level of civilization that they had all enjoyed.

The Portuguese Disruption

At the height of their prosperity the Swahili towns suffered an intervention from a European power which had disastrous effects on the Islamic civilization there, and for the western Indian Ocean trade on which it depended. This European power was Portugal, a small seafaring nation in the south west of Europe. Seeking to find a sea route to India, Vasco da Gama, one of their explorers, in 1498 passed through some of the Swahili towns, including Kilwa, Mombasa and Malindi. His report back to the king of Portugal about the wealth he had seen there led that monarch to send expeditions to seize as much of it as they could. With his superior weaponry, within ten years da Gama had looted and burned Kilwa and Mombasa. Malindi only escaped the same fate by allying with the Portuguese.

By 1509 the whole Swahili region was under the new invader's control. More than that, because of the crude measures they used to try to control and exploit the merchants who came from other parts of the Indian Ocean, the Portuguese reduced trade and commerce to only a fraction of what it had been previously. The effect of all this was the wiping out of Shirazi power, the final ruination of some of the towns, including Kilwa, and the breaking of most of the ties that had existed with the heartlands of Islam. Though the Swahili remained Muslims, the period of their high Islamic civilization had been brought to an end.

The Omani Era

The domination of the Portuguese lasted for around 150 years but was eventually eclipsed by Muslims from the Arabian Peninsula. At the height of its power Portugal had managed to win control of the Gulf region of Oman but when the Omanis managed to eject them some of the cities on the East African coast asked for their help to expel the Portuguese from their own area. Over the next fifty years, one by one Zanzibar, Pemba, Pate, Mombasa and the other coastal towns north of present-day Mozambique came under Omani control. The last Portuguese stronghold in that region, the massive Fort Jesus in Mombasa, fell in 1698.

The Omani era was a time of revival for the towns of the Swahili coast, though they never reached the level of prosperity they had enjoyed before the coming of the Portuguese. Trade links were re-established with the lands of the western Indian Ocean and there was fresh immigration of Arabs from Oman, and Persians from Shiraz which further strengthened the influence of Islam. During the eighteenth century the effectiveness of Omani control over the area was lessened by the individual towns' desire for their independence and by a power struggle between different Omani factions, but this changed in the nineteenth century when a strong and astute ruler came to power.

This man was Sayyid Sa'id bin Sultan. Having come to the throne in Muscat, the capital of Oman in 1806, Sa'id built up his power. He strengthened his position through a shrewd strategic alliance with the British. Having once been one of the leaders in promoting the slave trade worldwide, Britain was now trying to have it abolished and hoped that in Sa'id they would find an ally to stop the seaborne slave trade in the western Indian Ocean. Once Sa'id had secured his position in Oman against local enemies, he set about using his small but powerful navy to impose control over his East African possessions, and by 1835 he had overcome all rivals there. So important did his East African territories become to him that, in 1840, he moved his capital from Muscat in Oman to Zanzibar.

Sa'id developed a simple but effective way of ruling. He left the rulers of the various settlements to themselves as long as they recognized his overlordship and paid the 5% tax he levied on all imports and exports. He made it his policy to encourage Indian merchants and bankers to settle in Zanzibar giving full religious toleration to Hindus, and also to Shia Muslims. Indians played an important part in creating the wealth of Sa'id's empire. It was often they who administered his system of taxation and provided the finance for an increasing number of Arab/Swahili caravans that began to venture beyond the coast and along the trade routes into the interior.

Under Sa'id Zanzibar became the main centre for East African trade. To it were brought beads, guns and manufactured goods from India, Europe and America and through it were channelled the produce of East and Central Africa, principally, at that time, ivory and slaves. Sa'id also decided to make large tracts of the islands of Zanzibar and Pemba into plantations for growing cloves. The need for labour in them further stimulated the demand for a regular supply of slaves from the interior.

Chapter 26

Muslims Come to the Interior of East Africa

Early Contacts

Before the nineteenth century the traders and merchants of the Swahili coast had made little attempt to penetrate the interior of East Africa. The trade routes that existed throughout that region were operated by tribes like the Chagga and Kamba, who operated between the Kenyan Rift Valley and the coast around Mombasa, and the Nyamwezi who moved between Katanga and the coast opposite Zanzibar. The Yao, from their home at that time in southern Mozambique, ranged between the Congo and the coast near Kilwa. The merchants of the coast had been content to let these tribes bring the goods to them. However, owing to the success of Seyyid Sa'id in promoting international trade, the increasing demands of the European and American market for commodities like ivory, and the ready availability of credit from Indian financiers, increasingly Swahili and Arab traders began to think it worthwhile to equip their own caravans and travel inland.

The primary motivation of the Muslim Arabs and Swahili who moved into the interior was to become rich rather than to occupy territory or to spread their religion. Away from the coast they were dependent on the goodwill of the local chiefs for their personal safety and for access to the goods they wanted. They were usually welcome visitors because of the goods that they took with them, cloth, beads, guns and ammunition. In return, what the coastalists wanted most was ivory, but alongside this was the need for a means of transporting it back to the coast.

The readiness of coastal traders to purchase slaves for this purpose, and then to sell them at a profit on the coast, and the availability of guns, encouraged chiefs to provide these slaves, mainly by attacking and capturing weaker people. As a result, in this period the slave trade in East Central Africa increased, all the more so when labour came to be needed for the clove plantations of Zanzibar and Pemba.

Though the inland people who joined the retinue of these Muslim traders did tend to adopt the language and the dress of the coast as well as some elements of their religion, there is little evidence that the traders made any great attempt to spread Islam among the people of the interior with whom they came in contact. However, there is evidence that the culture of the coast was beginning to make an impression. For instance, David Livingstone, visiting the Yao Chief Mataka, east of Lake Malawi in 1866, found him dressed in Arab clothing. Livingstone also noticed houses built square in the style of the coast. He wrote, 'The Arabs are imitated in everything'.

There were some exceptions to the rule that the coastal traders did not seek political control in the interior. In the 1860 in the area of the Manyema in modern day Tanzania, a Swahili adventurer Muhammad bin Hamid, known as Tippu Tip, took advantage of the chaos his raids had caused there to establish an area under his control. In order to tie his personal supporters more closely to him he encouraged them to be circumcised and to profess Islam. A further important example of Muslim coastal traders establishing an area of control in the interior will be dealt with in the section about Malawi.

The Growth and Spread of Islam

An important impetus for a rapid growth in the number of people becoming Muslims in certain areas of the interior of East Africa seems to have been the increased intervention of European powers in the area, and its eventual colonization by them. One of the reasons for this was that Islam acted as rallying point for many people in the region in opposition to European domination. Europeans, in the persons of explorers and Christian missionaries, had been in the region since the mid-nineteenth century and, up till the 1880s, there is comparatively little mention of active hostility between them and the Muslims from the coast whom they encountered. This changed radically from around the mid-1880s when, during their 'Scramble for Africa', European powers, principally Britain and Germany, began to partition East Africa between themselves. In this process Britain broke long standing promises to the Sultan of Zanzibar and allowed the Germans to control what is now Tanzania. Britain itself laid claim to what is now Kenya and Uganda.

From that time European missionaries from Uganda to Malawi noted that they had begun to face what looked like a concerted attempt by the Swahili and their allies, coordinated by the Sultan of Zanzibar, to oppose European presence in the interior. In Buganda from 1884 the Muslim party at the royal court worked to turn the King there against the Christian missionaries and this led to the missionaries' temporary expulsion from the kingdom in 1889. In the region of inland Tanzania controlled by Tippu Tip the missionaries felt threatened. One missionary wrote, 'The Arabs have been commissioned by the Sultan of Zanzibar, to take possession of all the countries around the lake.' In the disturbances which followed many mission stations were abandoned. There was also strong resistance by the Swahili and their allies to European missionary and colonial domination in the area around Lake Malawi. This again will be dealt with in the section on Malawi.

Implications for the Development of Islam

There is evidence from many parts of the region that their determination to resist this European threat led chiefs and people allied to the Swahili to convert to Islam. Certainly, at this time Christian missionaries began to see Islam as a religious threat rather than the Swahili as political rivals.

Once European military superiority had overcome any resistance and colonial rule had been imposed, in many parts of East Africa the new conditions favoured the spread and development of Islam beyond the coastal strip. Swahili soldiers were often used by the colonialists to man their military garrisons. In Tanganyika the Germans adopted a system of indirect rule whereby their District Officers ruled through *jumbes* ('governors') who were Swahili Muslims recruited from the coast. As the whole region was opened up with road and rail links, Swahili Muslims were brought in as tax collectors, skilled workers, foremen and teachers. Improved communications and peaceful conditions also encouraged significant numbers of Swahili and Indian traders to move into the interior.

During the early colonial period there is evidence that Shaykhs belonging to the Brotherhoods, particularly the Qadiriyya and Shadhiliyya, were active in travelling around teaching, making converts and building up Islamic communities. As well as the successes of this proselytizing, many people were attracted to become Muslims by the social status of the Swahili. In the interior, though the Europeans held the highest positions of authority, Kiswahili became the *lingua franca* throughout East Africa. The Muslim Swahili who had long been looked up to for their level of civilization were often, in the colonial era, the visible representatives of the modern world with the skills and opportunities that it offered. Throughout East Africa people who aspired to emulate the Swahili style of life often adopted Islam as an important part of it. Till the present day the population of the East African coast from Somalia to northern Mozambique is predominantly Muslim and there are also significant numbers of Muslims inland.

Chapter 27

The Establishment of Islam in Malawi

Islam came to Malawi as part of the two-way traffic between the Muslim Swahili coast and the interior of East Central Africa. The first Muslims set foot in what is now Malawi probably around 1530, when Swahili Arab traders established a trading post at nearby Tete on the Zambezi. Though the coming of the Portuguese meant that the traders were expelled, up to the present day there are clans in that vicinity, known in Malawi as the Amwenye and in Zimbabwe as the Varemba, who still show signs of their ancient contact with Islam through their practice of circumcision, their refusal to eat pork and their Islamic sounding names. By the seventeenth century the area around Lake Malawi had links to the coast through two major trade routes, one terminating in Kilwa in present day Tanzania and the other in Angoche in present day Mozambique. One of the main tribes to work these routes, from their homeland, at that time, in southern Mozambique were the Yao.

Two series of events in the first part of the nineteenth century were important for the eventual establishment of Islam in Malawi. The first was from around 1830 when there were movements of Yao groups into the area around the southern end of Lake Malawi. The second, around the same time, was the increased number of traders from the coast who, encouraged by the opportunities for trade that were expanding under Sayyid Sa'id's rule in Zanzibar, started to travel into the interior of East Africa, and even set up trading stations there.

The Jumbes

In around 1860, or perhaps earlier, one of these Swahili traders, Salim bin Abdullah arrived in Nkhotakota, on the lake shore in central Malawi. Having asked the local Chewa chief, Malenga for land for the purpose, he established a trading station there with several villages for his personal followers. He was well armed and made a success of trading in the import of guns, gunpowder and cloth and the export mainly of ivory and then slaves. Through trade and diplomacy, he eventually became rich and powerful enough, following the death of Chief Malenga, to overthrow the paramount Chief Kanyenda and to get his sub-chiefs to acknowledge him as *Jumbe*, or Sultan. He and his three successors, known to history as the *Jumbes* of Nkhotakota, and claiming to represent the Sultan of Zanzibar, were able to set up a major entrepot and to build a fleet of dhows to cross the lake. This attracted much trade and many traders from the coast and all over the region.

The *Jumbes* were Muslims as were their personal followers and, though they do not seem to have made direct efforts to convert the local Chewa people, they did persuade their chiefs to send sons and nephews to the coast to be educated. Many of these young men were converted to Islam there and, when some in turn became chiefs or shaykhs, they were influential in persuading their own people to become Muslims. Even though the fourth *Jumbe* was deposed by the British in 1895, and most of the Swahili left Nkhotakota, by that time most of the chiefs in the area and many of the people were Muslims, a situation that remains till today.

A second Swahili trader to set up a base in Malawi was Mlozi bin Kazbadema. Modelling himself on the *Jumbes* further south, he set up a trading post near Karonga among the Ngonde people at the Northern end of the lake in about 1880 and declared himself to be 'Sultan of the Ngonde'. Though Mlozi was less successful than the *Jumbes*, and was killed in 1895 by the British in a trade war, there are still villages of Muslims in Karonga district today which date back to his time.

The Yao

By the time Yao groups moved into the Malawi area, from the 1830s onward, many of their people had had long contact with the coast, some having travelled and probably even lived there. When Swahili and Arab traders began to travel into the area of Lake Malawi, using the trade routes already established, it was with some of the Yao chiefs that they cooperated. Sometimes they would stay in the chiefs' villages, providing them with guns while their hosts procured the commodities they were looking for, particularly ivory and slaves. From this period onward there is evidence that the people from the coast were having an influence on the way local people dressed, the way they built their houses and boats and even the crops they planted. Eventually some of them, especially from among the chiefs, took on the religion of their Swahili partners and began to declare themselves as Muslims.

Though there would have been earlier conversion of some Yao people, especially among those who had been to the coast, the first of their chiefs to convert to Islam, was probably Makanjira III, around 1870. In 1876 a British traveller noted a school at his court where children were being taught the Qur'an by a Muslim teacher, or *mwalimu*. Literate Muslims from the coast were also used by chiefs as advisers and secretaries to handle their communications with their trading partners. By the end of that decade, Makanjira's powerful neighbours, Chiefs

Jalasi (Zarafi) and Mponda had followed his lead and converted to Islam. Much of the written evidence for the spread of Islam during this period comes from Christian missionaries, who arrived in the region some years after the Yao. It is likely that they underestimated how strongly Islam had already taken hold. Certainly, in Mponda's town Catholic White Fathers were surprised to find that, by 1891, there were twelve Qur'anic schools, *madrassas*, each with its own teacher, and to witness the month of Ramadan being observed.

European Opposition

It was Christian missionaries and their commercial allies who were the first Europeans to come to Malawi. They were strongly influenced by the ideas of David Livingstone whose vision was to put an end to the traffic in slaves and to prepare the way for 'Christian civilization' by establishing what he called 'legitimate' commerce. The Yao chiefs as well as the *Jumbe* in Nkhotakota and Mlozi, along with the Swahili who were their trading partners and advisers, feared that the trading patterns that the British wished to promote would be a threat to them and to their own way of trading. Their fears were justified. In Karonga, a war over trade broke out in 1887 between Mlozi and a Scottish trading company, the African Lakes Company.

When the British missionaries and their allies in Parliament helped to persuade the British Government in 1891 to declare Nyasaland a Protectorate, the administration set up there under Sir Harry Johnston used its military power to support the Scots and defeat Mlozi. Johnston also set about imposing British authority, by force, over the Yao chiefs whom he saw as responsible for the slave trade. Many of them, including Makanjira,

Kawinga, Mponda and Jalasi, resisted. It took a series of military campaigns which lasted till 1895 before they were finally subjugated.

Chiefs and Shaykhs

The military defeat of the Yao who had resisted colonial rule, the flight or detention of the leading chiefs, and the withdrawal of the majority of the Swahili traders back to the coast, did not however result in a weakening of Islam among many of the Yao groups. On the contrary, in the period that followed conversion to Islam became much more common. One explanation for this is that, in order to tie their subjects more closely to them, Muslim Yao chiefs added Islamic elements, like full circumcision and some instruction in Islam, to the traditional male *lupanda* initiation ceremony, creating a revised version known as *jando*. This meant that for those who underwent the ceremony, becoming an adult Yao was accompanied by identification with Islam. This has contributed to the close association between being Yao and being Muslim that has long been characteristic in Malawi, though of course not all Yao are Muslims.

While *jando* might have been the doorway for many Yao people into identifying themselves as Muslims, the people who were responsible for building up the practice of the religion were the religious leaders known as the shaykhs and *amwalimu* (from Arabic *mu'alim*, teacher). The earliest of these Muslim missionaries may have included Swahili but the most famous of them were certainly Malawians, mostly Yao, but sometimes Chewa. Among the most prominent were Abdullah bin Haji Mkwanda (1860-1930) and his pupil Thabit bin Muhammad Ngaunje (1880-1930). These men and others, some of whom had a high level of Islamic education from the Coast, travelled through or settled in areas where there were Muslims. They gave instruction about Islamic practice and belief, taught how to transliterate Arabic in order to recite the Qur'an, established mosques and gave certificates or *ijazas* to young men whom they trained up as shaykhs and *amwalimu*. The religious teachers cooperated with, and were enthusiastically supported by the chiefs and it was often the chiefs' sons and nephews who were taken on for special training by the shaykh or sent to the Coast for further studies. The chief was regarded as the father of the village and the shaykh as the head of the mosque.

Islamic Practice in this Period

By the end of the first decade of the twentieth century, Islam was becoming firmly established in many of the areas ruled by Yao chiefs, particularly in the present day Mangochi and Machinga districts, as well as in parts of Nkhotakota. In these areas most villages would have their own prayer houses, or even mosques to which a muezzin would call the people to the five daily prayers. On Fridays many would attend the obligatory noon prayer at the main mosque, which was almost invariably in the chief's village. There a sermon would be read by a shaykh or *mwalimu*. Ramadan would be observed each year, with varying degrees of strictness, as a time of fasting and increased religious scrupulousness. Both *Eid ul-Fitr,* at the end of Ramadan and *Eid ul-Adha*, the Feast of Sacrifice, would be celebrated. Strict Muslims would avoid intoxicants and most would keep Islamic dietary laws, avoiding the eating of pork and other prohibited animals and refusing to eat any animal that had not been killed in the approved manner. Many men would wear the cap and robe in the style of the coast to show their Muslim identity.

Certain traditional customs were altered under the influence of Islam. In addition to changes to the initiation rituals mentioned above, the periodic offerings that had traditionally been made for the spirits of the departed survived in an Islamized form and with an Islamic name *sadaka* (*sadaqa*). At this ceremony the community and the family of the deceased, in the presence of a shaykh or *mwalimu,* would share a meal and pray for the spirit of the departed. With regard to marriage, divorce and inheritance though, it was traditional rather than orthodox Islamic custom that was followed.

A further stimulus to increasing the number of Muslims and the development of some of the features which characterized the way Muslim communities in Malawi practised their faith was the activities of the Shadhiliyya and Qadiriyya Brotherhoods, or *tariqas*. Both came to Malawi via Zanzibar and the East Coast, the Shadhiliyya from about the first decade of the twentieth century and the Qadiriyya, which eventually became the stronger, by about 1920. By the 1930s most shaykhs were associated with one or other of the *tariqas*. These shaykhs introduced some of their practices which became widely popular among Malawian Muslims. Perhaps the most noteworthy was *sikili,* related to the Arabic *dhikr* (remembering God by repeating his names and attributes). In its typical form in Malawi this was a set of rhythmical movements accompanied by controlled breathing, which could be performed at mosques, during festivals, at weddings and, with the Qadiriyya, at funerals. Another popular practice that they introduced was the use of flags and banners.

One other significant factor in the spread and development of Islam in Malawi was the contribution of Muslim Asians who from the earliest colonial times settled as traders in towns and trading centres throughout the country. Though they followed the Hanifite school of law and the Malawian Muslims were associated with the Shafiite one, and while they remained socially separate from Malawian Muslims, they supported them in their attempts to build up their religion, particularly by providing resources for the building of mosques. They often also provided with employment many Malawian Muslims who moved with them as they dispersed around the country and in this way promoted the spread of Islam beyond its regions of origin.

While the policy of the Colonial Government was to try to remain neutral in matters of religion, the establishment of Islam that has been described was accomplished in the face of determined competition and opposition from the Christian missionary churches. Although the presence and activities of the missionaries, especially their control of education, did much to inhibit the spread of Islam, even among the Yao, beyond the areas where Islam had already been established, the churches proved relatively powerless to win over people who had chosen to be Muslims. The 1931 Nyasaland Government Census reckoned that Muslims constituted 8.4% of the country's population, though this may well have been an underestimation. By that time Muslim communities with their distinctive Islamic way of life and identity were firmly established.

Chapter 28

Education and Revival

Muslims and Western Education

One very significant choice that the overwhelming majority of Muslims made during the colonial era concerned education. During this period, if they wished their children to have schooling, two avenues were open to Muslim parents or guardians. The first was the Islamic education available from the shaykhs and *amwalimu* at the *madrassas* that they supervised, where their children would be taught mainly to transliterate Arabic and recite the Qur'an. The second was that of western education, which along with promoting Christianity, offered literacy, numeracy and technical skills. This sort of schooling could give access to positions of influence, prestige and relative prosperity as teachers, clerks, technicians and minor government officials in the wage-earning sector of the colonial economy.

The Muslim communities almost unanimously rejected the option of western education because, in the colonial era, it was offered almost exclusively by the Christian missions, who used the education they offered to promote the Christianity of their own denomination. Muslims, with justification, regarded the teaching, and the whole environment of the Christian schools as being hostile to their faith and as something which could take their children away from their families, their culture and their religion. That not all Muslims rejected western education for itself is made clear by representations by Muslim chiefs in 1916 and 1928 to have the Government provide schools for Muslim children, by attempts by individual

Muslims to provide western education in the 1940s and the setting up of the Central Body for Muslim Education in the mid-1950s to control and encourage Muslim education free of Christian influence. However, in spite of these initiatives very few Muslims in the colonial period took advantage of western education, and those who did sometimes gave up their Islamic faith.

Their boycotting of Christian controlled western schooling had significant social and economic costs for Malawi's Muslim communities. As the wage-earning sector of the colonial economy expanded and new opportunities opened for those who possessed western education, Muslims found themselves at a disadvantage. Though some prospered as traders, businessmen and skilled workers, the majority of Muslims in the waged economy were limited to lower paid jobs. As a result of this in Malawi in colonial times Malawian Muslims tended to be marginalized both socially and economically, a legacy that many of their descendants still bitterly resent today.

Independence

One of the important factors behind a revival of Islam in Malawi was a change in educational policy shortly before Malawi gained Independence in 1964. The majority of Muslims having supported his Congress party in the struggle for Independence, when he came to power, the first Prime Minister, then President, Dr Kamuzu Banda set out to fulfil a manifesto pledge to make education accessible in areas where Muslims predominated. To help to bring this about, having promised to put an end to what he called 'the marriage between religion and education', in 1962 he put control of the school curricula and pupil admissions into the hands of a Government Department of Education. In spite of the changes which followed,

Christian influence over the school system still remained strong and Muslims' reluctance to commit their children to it was overcome only slowly. However, from this time on, a growing number of young Muslims did pass through primary and secondary schools and eventually, when it became available, to tertiary education. Much of the credit for this has to go to the Muslim Association of Malawi which had developed from the Central Body for Muslim Education and claimed to be an umbrella organization representing all Malawi's Muslims. Through its Youth Committee and with the help of some of Malawi's Asian Muslims, during the 1970s it not only promoted *madrassa* education but also sponsored the education of Muslim pupils in primary and secondary schools on a significant scale. Their efforts helped to increase the number of western educated Malawian Muslims who would play an important part in the development of Muslim communities and the increasing prominence of Muslims in national life that happened in the last quarter of the twentieth century.

For these young Muslims possession of western education opened up new economic and religious horizons. Academic qualifications gave them the key to salaried, managerial and professional posts, the pioneers acting as powerful role models. In the realm of religion, literacy in English gave them direct access to information about orthodox Islamic belief and practice. Furthermore, opportunities to travel to international Islamic conferences, and in some cases even to study in Muslim countries, brought some of them into closer contact with the wider Islamic world. All these developments led them to conclude that, not only were Muslims in Malawi socially and economically disadvantaged, but also that their practice of some aspects of Islam there differed from what they themselves had come to understand as the Islamic ideal. Along with this realization came a determination to bring about what they saw as a revival within Malawi's Muslim communities, in terms of social and economic development and religious reform.

Revival and Development

An important impetus for this revival came in the form of an injection of finance and expertise from the Gulf Region of the Middle East. From 1982 until 1990 the main player was the African Muslims Agency, a progressive propagation and development organization, with its headquarters in Kuwait. Through its professional administrators the Agency cooperated with the Muslim Association of Malawi and some of the growing number of young, western educated and committed Malawian Muslims who were ready, willing and able to use its finance, help and guidance to further the development, well-being and religious reform of Malawi's Muslim communities.

By the 1980s a revival of Islam in Malawi began to flourish in ways that, by design, were very apparent both to Muslims and to wider Malawian society. A very obvious sign of the presence of the religion in Malawi, especially in the Southern Region, was the rapid construction of impressive new mosques, many of them prominently situated near main roads and built with money mostly from the Middle East. This, along with the refurbishment of many existing mosques, and the establishment of yet others sponsored by Muslim Asian families, set out to give confidence to Muslims, and notice to non-Muslims, of the presence and vitality of Islam in the nation.

Most of the new mosques had *madrassas* built beside them, set up to teach the Qur'an, *Hadith*, Jurisprudence and Arabic language with the aim of building up Islamic knowledge, along orthodox rather than traditional lines, particularly among its young people. Funding from the African Muslims Agency provided for the setting up in Blantyre of a centre for higher Islamic studies. Staffed by highly qualified expatriate teachers, many from Sudan, it offered not only Islamic teaching but also education that would lead to Malawi Certificate of Education qualifications. Along with five other centres, it worked to improve the knowledge and competence of *madrassa* instructors through in-service training, and to provide successful students with qualifications to study abroad.

Throughout the decade numbers attending *madrassa* education increased. Sometimes in predominantly Muslim areas local schools, whoever the proprietor, were claimed after hours for *madrassa* classes such was the demand. The 1980s also saw a proliferation of Islamic literature available in Malawi, mostly in English and Chichewa. Apart from translations of the Qur'an into these languages, there was also a wide range of booklets explaining and commending the beliefs and practices of Islam.

In this decade Muslims intensified their efforts to ensure that their young people improved their chances of gaining access to higher levels in society. This was apparent in the number of schools under Muslim proprietorship, and the number of bursaries granted to Muslim children to study at any primary and secondary school. The Muslim Students Association, set up in Malawi in 1982, and reformist in outlook, was particularly effective in carrying out its aims of encouraging Muslims in the national education system to learn about the beliefs and practices of their faith and to retain their religious identity in what was still a predominantly Christian environment.

Reactions

These developments, and the speed with which they were taking place, within a section of society which had previously had a low profile and was widely perceived to be non-progressive, brought a variety of responses. President Banda's government, while emphasizing its commitment to a policy of freedom of worship, was wary of any links being formed with Islamic countries, especially those with a record of exporting Islamic revolution. It consequently imposed some restrictions on travel and also kept developments within Malawi's Muslim communities under close watch. Some leaders of Christian churches interpreted the new assertiveness among Muslims as aggressive and expressed an anxiety, shared by some sections of the wider society, that activism might eventually lead to militancy.

Perhaps the most determined opposition to some of the efforts of the reformist Muslims was led by a section of the traditional *Ulama*, especially from the Qadiriyya Brotherhood. The traditional *Ulama* had up till then been regarded as the religious leaders of the Muslim communities and the authorities on matters of religious belief and practice. They felt challenged by the teaching of the reformers about what they claimed was proper Islam and the reformers' criticism that some of the practices that were part of the Yao Muslim tradition and way of life were un-Islamic innovations. Consequently, they put up a spirited resistance and defended their own position vigorously. One way they did this was to turn the charge of innovation against the reformers. They did this by claiming that it was the reformers who were putting aside long-established Islamic practices, and by so doing were destabilizing the Muslim communities.

Chapter 29

A Muslim President, 1994-2004

Muslims were both involved in and affected by the results of the major changes in the life of the nation brought about by the process which secured multi-party democracy and put an end to the rigidly authoritarian rule of Dr Banda. The call of the Catholic Bishops in May 1992 for an end to Government corruption, incompetence and abuse of human rights was immediately supported by the Muslim Association of Malawi. Along with representatives of most of the Christian denominations, the business community, trade unions and the legal profession, they helped to establish, and participated fully in the Public Affairs Committee (PAC) which was largely instrumental in securing the referendum that in 1993 endorsed multi-party democracy.

The major political parties that emerged to contest the election that followed were based largely on regional affiliation. The United Democratic Front (UDF) which had its stronghold in the Southern Region, where the Yao form a substantial minority and the majority of Muslims are to be found, was led by Bakili Muluzi, himself a Yao Muslim. During the election campaign, for the first time since the colonial era, Islam was openly politicized. Some of Muluzi's opponents tried to use the fear of Muslim domination to dissuade the electorate from voting for his party, but at the polls the UDF gained massive support from Muslims and non-Muslims alike in the populous Southern Region. This ensured that they would form the largest party in Parliament and that Malawi would have a Muslim President.

Changes

One change brought about by democratization, which had significance for Muslims, as for all Malawians, was the removal of a culture of fear-induced conformity that had characterized the Banda regime. This, along with the new government's policies which emphasised civil liberties and freedom of speech, meant that all groups in society, including Muslims, were much freer to express their identities, their ambitions and their claims. Certainly, in the new Malawi, and with a Muslim president, Muslims and various indicators of Islamic influence gained a higher profile. While Christians still dominated the government, parliament, the civil service, the educational system, the legal establishment, the diplomatic corps and the security services, an increased but not disproportionate number of top posts came to be held by Muslims. *Eid ul-Fitr* was recognized as a national holiday. Wearing the *hijab* became increasingly popular among both African and Asian Muslim women, a practice that had been frowned upon during the Banda era.

With the Muluzi administration there was also a trend toward the setting up of new non-governmental organizations and a decentralization of control among those which already existed. Qadiriyya Muslims set up the Quadria Muslim Association of Malawi, alongside the existing Muslim Association of Malawi, a development that would have been discouraged in President Banda's time for bringing 'confusion'. In 1995 the Muslim Association of Malawi set up a *Halal* Department to certify foods that could be eaten by Muslims. In 1999 the Association established its Islamic Information Bureau. In 2001 Radio Islam was set up. At an international level, diplomatic and economic ties were established with Islamic countries such as Libya, Malaysia, Kuwait, Sudan and the United

Arab Emirates. Presidential visits were exchanged with several of their Heads of State and substantial amounts of economic support for Malawi was promised from some of these countries, though not all of it was delivered.

Education and Development

One major feature of this period was the determination of Muslims and their leaders to open up further opportunities for education and development and to build up the ones which already existed. This was accompanied by a proliferation of organizations with this aim, with funding from inside the country and from abroad. An account of three of the many will give an idea of their activities and their impact.

The Islamic Zakat Trust which had been registered, in the Banda era in 1988, became very active with strong involvement of some of Blantyre's Asian Muslim community. Its stated aim was to use *zakat* contributions in order to provide scholarships and bursaries to needy Muslim youth, to enable them to become self-reliant and to contribute, themselves as *zakat* payers, to the development of their own communities, and also to the building up the nation. In cooperation with the Muslim Association of Malawi the Trust, through its Islamic Zakat Fund, gave sponsorship to many young Muslims who because of it were able to access secondary and tertiary education in Malawi, and by 2000, in universities abroad. It was also behind the setting up of Radio Islam.

The Lilongwe Islamic Movement was also very active in this era. It had been established, also in President Banda's time, by members of the Muslim Asian community in that city to alleviate poverty and promote *madrassa* education and development of Malawi's Muslim youth in the Central and Northern Regions of the country. The organization insisted that their pupils should attend school for western education in the mornings. In the afternoons they attended their *madrassas,* which by 2004 numbered around 250. Some of the successful students were sent for further studies to the Blantyre Islamic Centre or to South Africa, where the organization had strong connections.

Munazzamat Dawah Islamia is an international organization with branches in many countries. Its Malawi Mission was started, with a Sudanese director, in 1996. As well as running *madrassas,* by 2004 it had built and was administering four well equipped secondary schools, two for girls and two for boys. With their own entrance examinations, help in finding scholarships for needy Muslim pupils, yet open to all, and with qualified Muslim and non-Muslim staff, the schools presented their pupils for the full range of Malawi School Certificate of Education examinations. By 2004 a good proportion of former pupils, both girls and boys had gone on to colleges or universities in Malawi and beyond, many supported by scholarships from the Islamic Zakat Fund.

Through these and many similar organizations in Malawi, an increasing number of Muslim pupils and students were achieving a higher standard of education than the previous generation, and were doing so in an environment that built up and reinforced their faith. With this, many more of them gained access to more highly skilled jobs and managerial and professional positions while still keeping, and indeed displaying their Islamic identity. Because of this many younger Muslims were encouraged to raise their ambitions about what they could themselves achieve. However, especially in the more rural areas, there were still some Muslims who had reservations that these developments, even where offered in an Islamic environment, might come with the danger of their children becoming somewhat estranged from them and their long held religious and social traditions.

Malawi's Muslims and Wider Society

While relations between Muslims and non-Muslims remained generally harmonious, and Muslims were well integrated within Malawian society, four incidents during President Muluzi's terms of office shed a light on the position of Muslim communities in Malawi, and their perception of it.

The first was a *fatwa* (binding declaration) on 'Anti-Islamic Propaganda Machineries' issued in August 1998 by the Muslim Association of Malawi to the Government, all political parties, the media, civil society groups and all mosques. It described itself as an 'early warning' against what its writers perceived as the continued prejudiced defamation and negative stereotyping of Islam and Muslims, particularly by political opponents and large sections of the media, as well as the apathy and inactivity of the government in the face of it. Pointing out that having a Muslim president did not make Malawi an Islamic state and repudiating the claims that Muslims had this as a political agenda, the writers of the *fatwa* made an appeal, not for exemption of Muslims from criticism, but for balance and fairness.

Specifically, the *fatwa* appealed to the government for protection against defamatory claims that Muslims were trying to Islamize Malawi, to politicians not to use Muslims as 'a punchbag' or treat them as, 'second class citizens in their own country', to the press that they should avoid identifying the religion of Islam with terrorism and fundamentalism, and should report even-handedly, and to the general public that they should seek advice from qualified Muslims before making pronouncements. It appealed to all in society to think of themselves as Malawians first and then as members of their faith communities, and to Muslims at all times to exercise restraint, endurance and self-control.

The second concerns the 1999 election campaign. Despite the plea in the *fatwa* of the previous year, the election campaign politicized Islam once more when opponents claimed that the President had used foreign money to further an Islamist agenda. What was different from 1994 was that in the aftermath of the President's re-election there was in the Northern Region a series of attacks on mosques and on people from the Southern Region. Though this hostility was mainly directed at the UDF it was Muslims who, fairly indiscriminately, bore the brunt of it. The national Muslim leadership successfully dampened down any danger of a violent reaction. However, the fact that the violence had taken place, what they saw as a lack of urgency in the response of the police and the lukewarm condemnation of the attacks from the majority of Malawi's Christian church leaders added to Muslims' perception of the hostility of other elements in society, and of their own lack of security.

A third incident came from an attempt by the Government Department of Education in 2000 to replace, at secondary school level, the study of Bible Knowledge with that of Religious and Moral Studies, which included teaching about Malawi's three major religious traditions, Christianity, Islam and African Traditional Religions. The process which led to this change had started in the Banda era and the proposed syllabus, having been developed by educationists from a variety of religious backgrounds, had gone through the regular channels. However, as the President and the Minister of Education were both Muslims at the time it was implemented, despite similar changes having been made at primary level, without opposition, in President Banda's time, this move was construed by sections of the Christian churches to be part of a plan to Islamize Malawi. They managed to make the issue so controversial and lobbied so hard that the President felt pressured into suspending the implementation of the new syllabus.

Muslims, on the other hand, had generally welcomed the change as at last giving their religion its rightful place within the secondary school system. When the new syllabus was suspended, some groups were only dissuaded from taking to the streets in protest by a combination of firm police action and the restraining influence of the Muslims' national leadership. Though a compromise was arranged whereby schools could choose which syllabus to teach, this incident once more confirmed the belief of many Muslims that what they saw as the Christian establishment would lose no opportunity to use their influence to keep them marginalized.

The fourth incident had a global dimension. In April 2000, as part of the United States' so called 'War on Terror', five Muslim foreign nationals residing in the city of Blantyre were arrested at the behest of the United States on the suspicion, later proved baseless, that they had links to the al-Qaeda movement. Despite court injunctions served in Malawi the five were illegally extradited to Zimbabwe, the President seemingly unable to prevent it. The reaction of sections of the Muslim community, especially from among the Qadiriyya, untypically, involved a certain amount of violence with the stoning and burning of some Christian churches, but also with buildings of the UDF and the Muslim Association of Malawi as targets of protest. For many non-Muslims these disturbances were taken as evidence for what they were ready to believe was the inherently violent nature of the followers of Islam. By many Muslims, on the other hand, it was perceived as evidence of the hostility of the United States and the Western World to Islam and Muslims everywhere.

While Malawi's Muslims were justifiably proud of their nation having a Muslim president, their reactions to it were generally cautious. There were occasionally complaints from some of them that the President did too much to court favour with the Christian Churches to the neglect of Muslim communities. They were conscious of the limits of the President's power, as witnessed by the outcome of the incidents concerning the new Religious and Moral Education syllabus and the al-Qaeda suspects. The President did not always enjoy the undivided support of the Muslim communities.

As the 1998 *fatwa* and the attacks following the 1999 election illustrate, many Muslims felt vulnerable in the face of the hostility of some sections of Malawian society, and their readiness to politicize anything that might look like Muslims trying to 'Islamize' the country. They were also aware that there would come a time when there would no longer be a Muslim President.

Chapter 30

Muslims in Malawi 2004-2020

Despite attempts by his party to change the constitution to allow him a third term of office, Bakili Muluzi's presidency ended in 2004. His hand-picked successor was a Christian who had a Muslim as his Vice-President and claimed to have more Muslims in his cabinet than had his predecessor. Indeed, since that time, though there has not been another Muslim President, the four successors to this office, from three different political parties, Bingu wa Mutharika, Joyce Banda, Peter wa Mutharika and Elias Chakwera, have all been careful not to alienate, but rather to try to attract Muslim voters. They have done this either by having Muslims as running mates or significant numbers of Muslims in their cabinets. They have made it their practice to send greetings to Malawi's Muslims on the *Eids* and on the birthday of the Prophet, and to attend, some in Muslim attire, or be represented, at the festival celebrations.

In return, the leadership of Muslim organizations make it very clear that they support the government of the day, whatever the party, and aim to work with it to promote the peace, development and well-being of the nation. Though individual Muslims can, and sometimes do, come out in support of one political party or another, the leadership are generally careful to stress that the organizations that they represent are strictly non-partisan. Though it has not completely disappeared, there has not been anything like the level politicization of religion that characterized the Muluzi era.

Education and Development

One major feature in this period has been the further progress that Muslim organizations have made in promoting the education of Muslim children, particularly girls. There is an even stronger awareness that education is the key to developing the nation and advancing their own place in it. Organisations that already existed have generally expanded their operations and ones new to the scene have joined them to promote and provide for *madrassa* schooling and primary, secondary and vocational education, with a strong emphasis on development. The support for this comes from within Malawi and from abroad and shows some of the cooperation that exists between African and Asian Muslims in Malawi and also the links that both groups have with Muslims in the wider world.

For example, in 2008 the Islamic Zakat Fund, with the assistance of the Islamic Development Bank, set up the Maone Vocational Training Centre to provide apprenticeships in different technical trades. This has the stated aims of helping young people to be self-reliant, to be able to support their families and their communities and to add to the pool of the nation's much needed skilled labour. The running costs of the Training Centre are met by *zakat* and other donations, mostly through the UK based Malawi Relief Fund. The Islamic Zakat Fund has also continued to expand its support for secondary pupils and also for students in colleges and universities in Malawi and in Islamic universities abroad, especially in Tanzania, Uganda and Sudan. Cooperating with the Muslim Association of Malawi and other partners, by 2018, the Fund claimed to have provided or found support for over 17,000 pupils at secondary and over 2000 students at tertiary level.

Those who sponsor the students and those who run the relevant organizations put great emphasis on the importance of people at each level using their qualifications for the good of the development of the whole of the nation. Muslim leaders claim that a much higher proportion of Muslim than non-Muslim graduates return to Malawi with their professional qualifications and work within the country on completion of their studies overseas.

Desire for a Muslim Friendly Society

Malawi's Muslims are basically well integrated into wider Malawian society. Many extended families contain both Muslims and non-Muslims. People share villages, towns, workplaces and political parties harmoniously and mourn and often celebrate together. Freedom of worship is fundamental to the nation's constitution and is unchallenged in practice. Nonetheless Muslims have made attempts to ensure that they can have a political and social environment that gives them space to express and uphold their Islamic identity, customs and values. Some aspects of this are particularly strong in districts like Mangochi and Machinga where Muslims form the majority of the population.

One example of this has been efforts to secure for Muslim women the right to wear *hijab,* in the form of a headscarf, in every situation. This right was granted to nurses in 2012. In 2017 the Muslim Association of Malawi pursued a court case which resulted in Muslim women being given the right not to remove their headscarves for driving licence photographs. In 2019 this provision was extended to passport photographs. The question of whether Muslim girls should have the right to wear *hijab* in all schools has been a source of contention. This has been the case particularly in Mangochi and Machinga where many Muslim girls attend schools run by Christian Churches. When the proprietors have insisted that their pupils conform to school rules about dress and not wear *hijab* this has occasionally led to confrontation and even disturbances. In some schools there has also been opposition from Muslim parents to the extension of timetables into the afternoon, as this would interfere with their children's *madrassa* classes which normally take place at that time.

Another issue which has been contentious has been the selling of pork in market places. Throughout the country Muslims have campaigned to stop this practice on the grounds that it is offensive to their religious sensibilities. It is an issue about which feelings can run high and when pork has been brought to a market some Muslims have sometimes taken direct action to prevent this happening. This has occasionally led to disorder, again particularly in areas where there is a Muslim majority.

At various times Muslim groups, along with some Christian ones, have lobbied against the indiscriminate use of condoms and the legalization of abortion. Muslim MPs have also lobbied in Parliament against gambling and against proposals to make polygamy illegal. All this on the grounds that what they are opposing is contrary to Islamic values.

There has been lobbying, particularly from Qadiriyya Muslims, to have the birthday of the Prophet, *Maulid ul-Nabi* recognized as a national holiday. This occasion is now marked annually in Malawi's cities by large parades and celebrations, known as *Ziyara,* which they organize. This proposal however does not have the support of all Muslims, as the more conservative Muslim Association of

Malawi do not think that it is justified by the Qur'an, the practice of the Prophet, nor the *Shariah*.

Related to Muslims' desire for them and their religion to be given fuller recognition in the life of the nation is the refusal of many of them to accept the results of National Censuses about the proportion of Muslims in the population. Though the 2018 Census put this at 13.8%, the Muslim Association of Malawi claims that its own figures show the proportion to be much higher, at around 35%.

In order to ensure that their concerns and the part that Muslims play in the life of the nation are all well reported and appreciated, Muslim organizations and individuals make good use of the media. Radio Islam continues as a broadcaster with high professional standards and along with the Islamic Information Bureau's website 'Malawi's Muslims', provides coverage of religious matters, education, development, politics, health, agriculture and other general news. Between these two outlets and the coverage provided by other national media outlets, Muslims and issues that concern them are highly visible. Many of the news items concern the charitable contributions Muslim individuals and organizations make, often for the benefit of the wider community, to famine and disaster relief, support for patients and health centres as well as for educational and developmental causes.

Unity in Diversity

One significant indication of how much more unites than divides Malawi's different religious communities is the work over the years of the Public Affairs Committee (PAC), in which Muslim and Christian leaders cooperate with the main civil society bodies.

In the area of politics, the PAC has been involved in promoting voter education, campaigning for electoral reform, calling for calm during elections, castigating individuals and organizations who have at any time tried to politicize religion, opposing Government interference with the Judiciary, conciliating between political parties, holding joint prayers for peace, and warning religious leaders against endorsing any one political party. In 2019-20 the PAC played an important role in bringing about the re-run of what the judiciary decided was an invalid election. In other areas the PAC has spoken out against what it has termed tribal and regional patronage, and against widespread and systemic financial corruption. It has also been involved in helping to resolve inter-religious conflicts such the issue of Muslim girls wearing *hijab* in Christian controlled schools.

One incident from 2020, involving an intervention of the PAC, illustrates not only some of the inter-religious tensions that can find expression in contemporary Malawi but also the level of good will and tolerance that exists to contain and help to resolve them. The incident had its origins in the erection of a poster by the Islamic Information Bureau on a prominent site in the city of Blantyre. Based on the Islamic teaching that the Qur'an is the fulfilment of the Bible, it invited Christians, having read the Old and New Testaments, to read what they termed, 'the Last Testament', namely the Qur'an. A conservative Christian group objected, on the grounds that this was a provocative message in what they claimed was a predominantly Christian country, and demanded that it be removed by the City Council. When this did not happen, the poster was vandalized which in turn provoked a reaction from the Muslim Association of Malawi, who threatened mass demonstrations.

In order to find a resolution to what was starting to look like an inflammatory situation the Government Minister of Civic Education called on the PAC to mediate. As a result of the negotiations that followed it was agreed that the poster would be reworded, urging people to read the Qur'an but without reference to the Bible, and that the Christian group should withdraw its statement about Malawi being a Christian country. Following this affair and that of the schoolgirls' headscarves, the PAC set up a taskforce to advance peaceful coexistence between religious groups.

Though in the many ways already described Malawi's Muslim communities are distinctive, this should not cloud the overall picture. Religious differences are by no means the most divisive in Malawian society. Ethnic and regional rivalries and the gap between the privileged and the poor are all much more so. All Malawians together face the same challenges of poverty, endemic corruption, donor dependency, pandemics, health and education services under strain, overpopulation, land degradation and lack of food security. They also share the same efforts to develop the country's human and natural resources with the hope that the nation can be peaceful, equitable and prosperous. The evidence is overwhelmingly that Malawi's Muslims are playing a full part in trying to bring this about.

Suggestions for Further Reading

Abadalati, Hammudah, *Islam in Focus*, American Trust Publications, Indianapolis, 1975.

Ali, Yusuf Abdullah (Translator), *The Meaning of the Holy Qur'an*, The Islamic Foundation, Leicester, 2003, (from which the quotations in this book have been taken).

Armstrong, Karen, *Islam, a Short History*, Phoenix, London, 2001.

Aslan, Reza, *No God but God*, new edition, Arrow: London, 2011.

Azumah, John, *My Neighbour's Faith: Islam explained for Christians*, Grand Rapids: Zondervan, 2008.

Bone, David S. (ed), *Malawi's Muslims, Historical Perspectives*, Blantyre: CLAIM-Kachere, 2000.

Clarke, Peter B., *West Africa and Islam: A Study of Religious Development from the 8th to the 20th Century*, 2nd edition, Edward Arnold: London, 1984.

Cragg, Kenneth, *The Call of the Minaret*, Oxford University Press, 1956.

Dawood, N.J. (Translator), *The Koran*, London: Penguin, 1997.

Denny, Fredrick Matthewson, *An Introduction to Islam*, 4th edition, New York: McMillan, 2010.

Esposito, John L., *Islam, the Straight Path*, updated 5th edition, Oxford University Press, 2016.

Fage, John D., (ed), *The Cambridge History of Africa*, vols. 2 and 3, Cambridge University Press, 2001.

Guillaume, Alfred, *Islam*, London: Penguin, 1956.

Hiskett, Mervyn, *The Course of Islam in Africa*, Edinburgh University Press, 1994.

Hitti, Philip K., *The Arabs, a Short History*, London: McMillan: London, 1996.

Mawdudi, Abu A'la, *Towards Understanding Islam*, The Islamic Foundation, 1996.

Rahman, Fazlur, *Islam*, second edition, University of Chicago Press, 1979.

Ruthven, Malise, *Islam in the World*, 2nd revised edition, Oxford University Press, 2000.

Watt, W. Montgomery, *Muhammad, Prophet and Statesman*, Oxford University Press, 1974.

Online Resources

www.ancient.eu (Ancient History Encyclopedia).

www.britannica.com (Encyclopedia Britannica).

www.clearQur'an.com (The Qur'an [translated]).

www.ingramcontent.com/pod-product-compliance
Lightning Source LLC
Chambersburg PA
CBHW021710230426
43668CB00008B/786